CW01660778

Bangkok street food

COOKING & TRAVELING IN THAILAND

Bangkok street food

COOKING & TRAVELING IN THAILAND

Tom Vandenberghe & Eva Verplaetse

PHOTOGRAPHY: Luk Thys
FOOD STYLING: Els Goethals

PAGE ONE

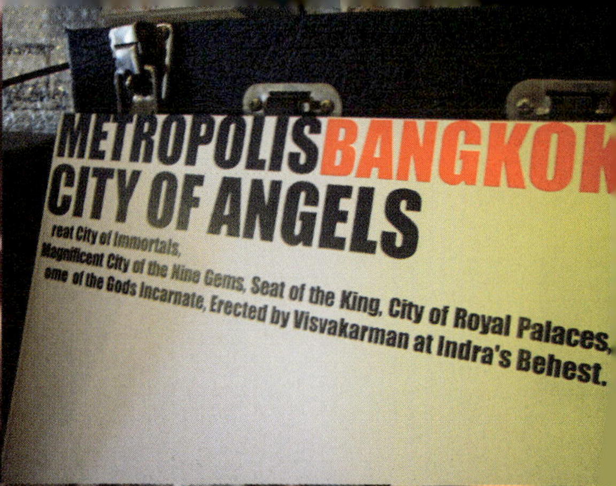

The amount and variety of street food in Thailand cannot be matched anywhere.

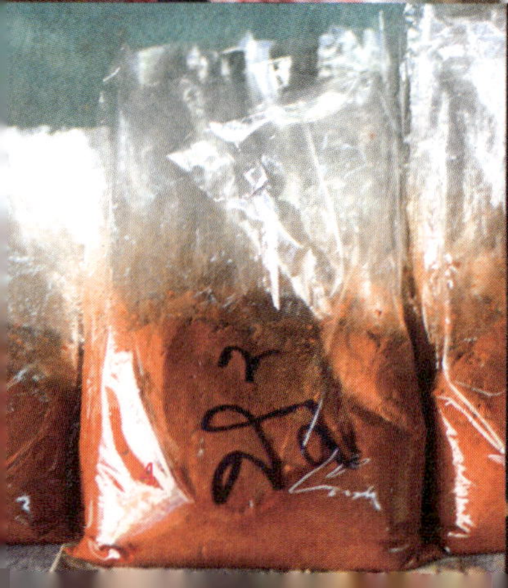

Content

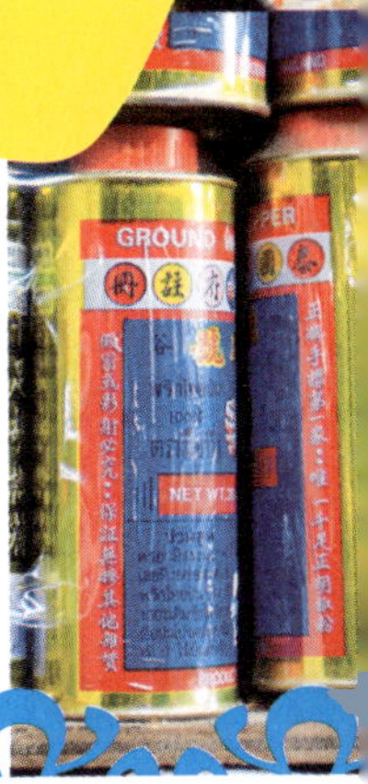

Introduction

In Thailand millions of people from all walks of life fill their stomachs at roadside food stalls or food markets on a daily basis. The streets literally turn into makeshift kitchens, pavements are occupied with small stools and fold down tables. The streets and footpaths have a different meaning from the West where they are just for walking and driving on. Here the space is divided up and used for the population to sit down and dine. To meet this demand, an army of street vendors works day and night, moving carts, setting out tables, cutting ingredients, cooking and cleaning. The amount and variety of street food in Thailand cannot be matched anywhere. The diversity, abundance and quality of ingredients are incomparable with any country in the world. With basic equipment these chefs of the streets turn their ingredients miraculously into all kinds of exciting food. If you're keen on learning about Thai culture the best way is to eat as locals do, you will be rewarded with a vibrant and delicious food culture.

Eating out in Thailand isn't something you do occasionally; it's something you do at least once a day, a part of daily social life. It happens continuously: on plastic chairs on a pavement, in a more upmarket restaurant, at a train station, on a beach or at a picnic in a park. Wherever there are people gathered, there will be someone cooking and an array of delicious dishes available. There's no better way to absorb the Thai ambiance than at a food market, where people get together to socialise, eat and drink. It's hard to tell which comes first. These makeshift kitchens can be found on any street corner, underneath flyovers in busy cities, on side-walks, anywhere that is convenient.

Since Thailand's social security system is still in its infancy, the street food business is often a safety net for people without income. There is the classic story of a woman who, after becoming a widow, starts selling noodle soup. A desperate way to make ends meet. Her delicious soup turns out to be a success on the street. After a while, she moves her business to a restaurant and becomes famous for her noodle soup. Or that of the student who sells pork sticks after school to be able to afford studying. Or the immigrant worker, selling papaya salad as an extra income, after he finishes planting rice in the north-eastern part of Thailand.

As the Thai standard of living is on the rise, supermarkets are substituting the traditional old markets and air-conditioned food courts are taking the place of street food vendors. There is a tendency towards higher hygiene standards, better and safer infrastructure. However, the concept of eating out on the streets is so deeply rooted and popular in Thai society that it's hard to imagine Bangkok will ever turn into a next Singapore where food courts are the standard and food hawkers are virtually banned from the streets. A lot of the famous Thai dishes actually originated on a street corner or at a food market and made it to the gastronomic world of food. That's why you can find the soul of Thai food on the streets, ready to be sampled by everyone with a culinary interest or a hungry stomach.

In the early days, the market was the core of the community and the only place to stock up on food. To make it easy for visitors, clever vendors started preparing take-away dishes at the market. They had to bring cooking utensils every day from their house to the market and back. Along the way they served the occasional customer and increasingly they equipped themselves as mobile cooking units. Instead of serving people at the market, they brought the market to the people.

One of the oldest forms of selling and transporting street food is by 'haph', a wooden stick with a woven basket attached on each side which resembles a large set of weighing scales. This ancient form of food hawking is still applied all around Thailand. With a 'haph', vendors can easily manoeuvre in the narrow streets, across bridges and on markets. The vendor would go from one place to another, from village to village, to sell his or her food; some of them even carry small chairs to seat their customers.

Another early means of bringing food to the people in the kingdom was by boat. The image of floating markets has become an icon of Thailand and a major tourist attraction. Thai society revolved around rivers and canals which provided fish, water and transport. The 'kuaytiạw rua' is a fully equipped cooking boat that peddled on rivers to vend noodle soup to people both on and along the river. Still today some noodle vendors in Bangkok put a boat in front of their shop to store their ingredients or cooking utensils, and to keep the memory alive.

Later, the bicycle found its way into the world of street food. Cycling from door to door, vendors made their own sounds to inform potential customers of their presence. With bells or a click from a wooden stick, some of them sang a specific song or whistled a tune. This way, people didn't need to come out of their house to look out for the arrival of their favourite food seller. Soon motorised vehicles were added to the list of vendor carts 'rot khem', from side-car motorcycles to customised pick-up trucks. Meals on wheels!

Thai people equipped themselves with mobile cooking units.

About Tom

When I first visited Bangkok in 1995, it struck me how eating, cooking and buying food is one of the main pass times up and down the country. It seems like everyone is constantly enjoying some kind of culinary pursuit. At any hour of the day you can indulge yourself with simple to elaborate dishes; it is possible to literally eat around the clock. When one place closes, another one opens up. Thai people eat more or less five light meals or snacks daily. They eat small portions at a time which is healthier and easier to digest than big lumps of meat and huge plates of food.

It took me some time to adapt and develop a real passion for authentic Thai cuisine. Like many travellers I ate in western-oriented Thai restaurants, where English menus decorate the tables. I didn't venture to the street food stalls at all. But that gradually changed. One of my first memories of authentic Thai food took place in a riverside restaurant in Bangkok. I tasted a fabulous spicy salad with prawns. The spiciness of Thai chillies combined with fresh and sour limejuice made my taste buds go wild. This dish blew me away! Back home I tried copying the dish to surprise my friends at a dinner party, hoping they would enjoy the same sensation.

A few years went by. Hundreds of experiments with Thai cooking in our own kitchen and a dozen or so food trips around the world later, my girlfriend Eva and I decided to quit our nine-to-five jobs to live in Thailand for a year. We didn't want to spend the entire year traveling, reading and hanging out, but felt the need to get something more out of our sabbatical.

I was working in a local travel agency in my home town and already had a passion for different types of world cuisine. In Thailand, cooking and enjoying food is such a nationally widespread obsession and ingrained in all aspects of culture. We decided to combine all those elements and devise a culinary tour, to explain Thai culture through Thai food to customers from Belgium and The Netherlands. A guided group trip with a focus on Thai food.

It was a perfect plan: a year of traveling, exploring Thai food culture and looking for great restaurants to take our groups to. At first it wasn't easy to find genuine Thai cuisine as we only knew the very basics of the language. After attending a course in spoken Thai, the culinary world gradually revealed its secrets to us. Things went pretty fast and before we realised it, we were waiting at Bangkok Airport for our first group of food-loving travellers to arrive. Our tours based on local and traditional dining establishments through Thailand had set off.

After introducing several groups to Thai and Vietnamese food culture, we set up a business in Belgium called 'Eetavontuur', which literally translates to 'Eating Adventure'. Our basic idea was the same as food hawking: share our knowledge of Thai cooking and to bring authentic Thai cuisine to people's doorsteps. We rented a space and equipped it as a cooking studio. Today we run a successful catering business and organise cooking classes for companies and private groups. When doing business, we stick to the Thai principle of fresh, high-quality products and loyalty to our customers.

eet avontuur

About this book

This book is the result of all our travels in and outside Bangkok and my experiences as a passionate Thai food chef in Europe. Its purpose is to provide you with an insight into the Thai street food culture and to share with you our authentic street food recipes.

We don't claim to have included in this book every available street food item in Bangkok. There is not only too much on offer, it's also a scene that is subject to perpetual evolution. New dishes find their way to the people, older ones disappear: the survival of the tastiest. Or better yet, the survival of the most popular. In this book we bring you a selection of traditional Thai street food dishes that are widely available and easy to stumble upon. And of a few classics that are not so easy to find but should be discovered before they disappear from the scene.

Vendor carts move from place to place, a street food scene today can be totally different next year. The addresses we mention in this book are places that have been around for many years. Most of them originally started on a pavement but already have turned into semi-restaurants. We wanted to make sure that whenever you look for these culinary hotspots in Bangkok, they are still there. Most dishes are widely available in many food markets and public places around Thailand. We hope this book will help you to recognise the dishes presented there and will function as a guide for visiting the addresses we are proud to mention.

Some of the recipes were disclosed to us by the vendors themselves. For others we had to rely on our experience and knowledge of Thai cooking. As many chefs in Thailand do not measure ingredients when cooking, you should allow some room for interpretation and do a lot of tasting while cooking. Just as Buddhism is finding a balance in life, cooking Thai food is all about finding the right balance between the five elementary tastes: sweet, sour, salty, bitter and spicy.

Identifying and grouping

For a first time visitor to Thailand, the abundance of street food is overwhelming and confusing. With some patience it's actually not as difficult as it seems to find your way through that culinary maze. First of all, each food hawker specialises in one kind of food. They all stick more or less to their own category of food as they need specialised utensils for preparing it. Vendor carts are not professional and fully equipped kitchens. They merely contain the necessary parts for preparing a certain type of dish.

To identify the food hawker and his or her food, you first have to take a look at the tools or equipment that he or she uses. To simplify this, we call it the hardware. Second, you look at the ingredients that are often displayed in a glass case or in a basket; this is what we will call the software. If you can identity the tools (hardware) and the ingredients (software), figuring out what type of food this vendor sells becomes easy. The hardware implies the cooking method.

We have categorised the recipes in this book according to the cooking method: grilled, boiled, steamed, fried, mixed and relishes. We also included a brief section of fruits, drinks and of ready-made dishes.

In Thailand the abundance of street food is overwhelming and confusing.

Index and cooking method

yang~

For more delicate foods, banana, coconut or pandan leaves are used as a wrapping.

Grilled (yang)

ย่าง

Grilling food vendors are a common sight on the streets of Bangkok. Generally and traditionally they use charcoal to grill their dishes. This adds a distinctive flavour to the food. You can compare it to our barbecue and it's just as popular. Sometimes the food is directly exposed to the heat but for more delicate foods like fish a wrapping is used. Banana, coconut or pandan leaves are usually preferred over aluminium foil. Not only does it look more attractive, the leaves help contain moisture, are naturally non-stick and flavour the food with their distinct scents and tangs. Remember though not to eat the wrapping!

Some food vendors have a small earthenware pot in which the charcoal is burning and a small grill on top. They use it when an order comes in. Others have a larger grill, more like our western barbecues, displaying their food while cooking.

Recipes

tom~

A large pot with liquid is boiling, waiting for an order to come in.

Boiled (tom)

ต้ม

When you see aluminium pots and a gas stove, you have to look at the glass showcase for the ingredients to determine what type of food this hawker is selling. The main categories are (noodle) soups, stews and the minced salads ('laab').

Some vendors have a wider range on offer, others specialise in just one but even then you can still customise it to your liking. Which kind of noodles do you prefer? What kind of meat? What extra ingredients would you like? Simply point to indicate what you want. In most cases a large pot with liquid (stock or water) will be kept close to boiling during the shift and is used when an order comes in.

Recipes

A classic Thai steamer is made of aluminium.

neung~

Steamed (neung)

นึ่ง

Steaming is in many situations preferable to boiling. The ingredients do not directly touch the liquid but are cooked by the vapour or steam that comes from the boiling liquid below. This preserves most of the nutrients, which makes it a much healthier way of cooking food. It goes without saying that the best result is obtained when the freshest possible ingredients are used. A classic Thai steamer is made of aluminium. It consists of a bottom layer for the boiling liquid, different levels or layers similar to racks for steaming the food and a top or lid. It comes in different sizes. Foods that require more steaming time will be steamed at the lower bottom or layer. Thai people will use this steamer to reheat or to keep food warm as well. You may find the typical Chinese buns ('salapao') in an aluminium steamer waiting to be sold. Steamed fish cake in banana cups ('ha mok pla') can be another option.

For smaller dishes like Thai dim sum ('khanom jeep'), street food vendors will use the small round bamboo steamers. They come in different layers as well, but do not have the bottom layer. They are placed over a cooking pot or wok filled with boiling liquid. Another famous dish that is mostly steamed in smaller bamboo steamers and presented that way on markets is the steamed small mackerel ('pla tuu'). For steaming sticky rice ('khao niaw') you will find steaming baskets (pyramid shaped) and a metal steaming pot for the liquid. To keep the steam inside, the pot is covered with a lid or a towel.

Recipes

page 45 ▪ **Thai dim sum** – khanom jeep – ขนมจีบ
47 ▪ **Steamed bun** – salapao – ซาลาเปา
70 ▪ **Steamed fish cake** – ho-mok-pla – ห่อหมกปลา
74 ▪ **Steamed small mackerel** – pla tuu neung – ปลาทูนึ่ง
127 ▪ **Sticky rice** – khao niaw – ข้าวเหนียว
128 ▪ **Sweet sticky rice with coconut and mango** – khao niaw mamuang – ข้าวเหนียวมะม่วง
133 ▪ **Pumpkin with custard** – sang khaya phak tong – สังขยาฟักทอง
149 ▪ **Steamed sea bass with lime dressing** – pla ka pong neung manao – ปลากะพงขาวนึ่งมะนาว

thod~

Most of the times, only one ingredient or component is cooked by deep-frying, to obtain the crispy texture in a dish.

Fried

The 'to fry'-section is divided into 3 categories: deep-fried, on a plate and stir-fried because the used hardware is very characteristic and easy to determine.

Deep-fried (thod) ทอด

Thai food has a very healthy reputation although deep-frying is used frequently. In defence of that reputation, most of the times only one ingredient or component is cooked by deep-frying, often to obtain that crispy texture in a dish. Portions are smaller and Thai people will try to counterbalance the fat with greens and/or fruit: yin and yang.

Deep-frying takes place in a large wok, sometimes with two handles and on a big gas stove. The latter is important because otherwise the temperature of the oil will drop too fast and the food will be greasy. If the oil is hot enough, deep-frying heats the moisture in the food, causing it to release steam. The outflow of steam prevents oil from seeping in. A large Chinese wire strainer is used to transfer and manoeuvring the food. This type of hawker will have a wire rack to place the deep-fried goods on to allow the grease to drain and to prevent it from becoming soggy.

Recipes

Fried on a plate

This is a somewhat in-between category. The food is fried, sometimes stir-fried but a special plate or equipment (e.g. for the coconut puddings) is used. The heat source is mainly a gas stove nowadays. Sometimes you can still stumble upon a vendor using a charcoal fire.

Recipes

Stir-fried (phat) ผัด

People tend to believe that all Asian food is prepared in a wok but only a minority of the Thai dishes need the wok as essential hardware. Sometimes a wok comes in handy for preparing a small amount of soup or to put the steamer on but that is not essential hardware. For the stir-fry dishes however, it is necessary to use a wok. The preparation takes up most of the time, all the ingredients need to be cut beforehand in bite-size pieces but once done, heat up some oil and quickly toss in your ingredients in the right order. Stir-fry until cooked, this should only take a few minutes because of the size of the ingredients. As a result, nutrients and taste are preserved. It's a quick and healthy way of cooking. The shape of the wok - the bottom being the hottest part, the sides less hot - allows the cook to put aside ingredients that are ready. An essential utensil is the spatula for tossing the food. When you see a hawker with a wok on a gas stove, you have to look at the ingredients to tell what this type of vendor will sell. Mostly a glass showcase is used.

Recipes

mixed~

One thing to remember is that in Thailand a 'yam' is usually spicy.

Mixed

This section includes 'yam', a spicy-sour salad with altering ingredients but mainly with a dressing based on fish sauce, lime juice, sugar and chillies and a variety of fresh herbs. If you're a health-conscious reader, you probably noticed that this list contains no fat, unlike most of our dressings. One thing to remember is that in Thailand a 'yam' is usually spicy! This section comprehends more than 'yam'; some dishes are pounded, some are merely composed, others have a different dressing. Therefore we decided to opt for the Thai meaning of 'yam', which is 'to mix'. When you see a wooden or clay mortar and pestle, you can be sure the eminent green papaya salad is sold there. Other hardware to look out for is a mixing bowl. Look at the ingredients displayed in the glass show case or on ice to determine what's on offer.

Recipes

A lot of Thai dishes are not complete without the specific dip or relish.

Relishes, dips and pastes

We put these into a separate category as a lot are made in advance. The secret of many dishes around the world lies in the preparation of subtle sauces, dressings and dips. Basic cooking techniques can be taught but really mastering a certain type of cuisine requires knowledge of that little extra that makes it truly authentic. A lot of Thai dishes are just not complete without the specific dip or relish that is served along with them.

Recipes

Ready-made dishes (khao kaeng)

ข้าวแกง

This book would not be complete without mentioning the hawker who sells ready-made dishes ('khao kaeng', literally 'rice and curry'). All dishes are displayed. It's easy; you only have to point at the dishes you want. A lot of the dishes are curry-based dishes or other ones that are more time-consuming to prepare.

pon la mai sod~

Chunks of ice are used to keep the fruit cool.

Fruits (pon la mai sod)

ผลไม้สด

Every morning when I wake up, I take a first good look out in the streets to see who's there and what's on offer to kill that morning appetite. I spot the fruit seller ('pon la mai sod') just next to the temple. Years ago in India I learned fruit is best eaten in the morning on an empty stomach. The fruit vendor already knows my preference and for 10 Baht, he professionally cuts up half a pineapple ('sapparot') into eatable chunks. He hands it to me in a small plastic bag with a bamboo skewer and smiles.

These vendors are on the move most of the time, going from one area to another. Common fruits to be sold are rose apple, green mango, pineapple, watermelon, cantaloupe and guava. Chunks of ice are used to keep the fruit cool. Usually two dips are on offer: a salt and sugar mixed with crushed chillies or a sweet-spicy dip with fish sauce. The latter typically eaten with green mango, the first with all kinds of fruit. It may not sound appealing but it's actually very tasty.

Other fruit vendors sell by the piece or by weight. Possible types of tropical fruit you might encounter are:
▪ Dragon fruit ▪ Custard apple
▪ Papaya ▪ Mangosteen ▪ Green mango
▪ Longan ▪ Starfruit ▪ Watermelon
▪ Guava ▪ Rambutan ▪ Jackfruit
▪ Pomelo ▪ Durian ▪ Sapodilla

dragon fruit

papaya

mangosteen

pomegranate

kreung deuum~

Beverages (kreung deuum)

เครื่องดื่ม

During your meal at a food stall, free water is provided. But the range of other beverages is wide. At most food stalls you can bring your own drinks. You can easily recognize the vendor who sells fruit juice and smoothies by the large amount of fruit and at least one blender. The most common drinks are orange juice ('naam som'), watermelon juice ('naam tengmo'), pineapple juice ('naam sapparot'), coconut juice ('naam ma phrao') en lime juice ('naam manao). In most cases, these drinks are mixed with crushed ice ('naam kheng') and milk, a bit similar to our milkshakes. If you fancy a smoothie without milk, just put the word 'pan' after your order. Often other refreshments, such as coke, soda water and beer are sold too.

One of my favourite drinks in Thailand is sugarcane juice ('naam oy'). It tastes sweet and it's the perfect thirst quencher. This vendor will carry a special machine to squeeze out the juice from the cane.

Herbal drinks are common as well. Look out for the large glass cylinders that contain unfamiliar fluids. Fine examples are lotus root juice ('naam rak bua'), longan juice ('naam lamyai') and juice extracted from the leaf of the land lotus ('naam bai buabok').

Millions of people fill their stomach every day at roadside food stalls or food markets.

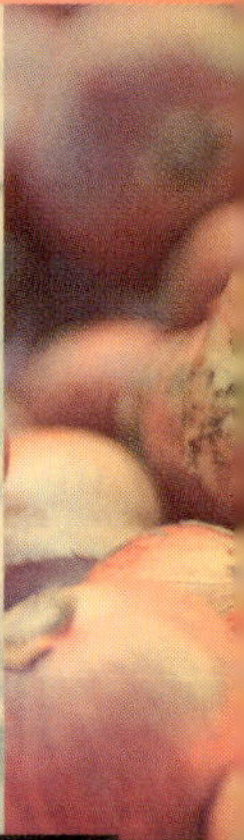

Tom's story

In the morning

In Bangkok, the Thewet area (A) is our home away from home. For years it has been our base for our culinary explorations of South-East-Asia. The area has friendly people, great food and is located in one of the oldest and definitely one of the more authentic of Bangkok's markets.

In Thailand life starts early every day. I love to get up at dawn. The sunlight is soft and almost artificially beautiful. It's still quiet but at the same time there are already a lot of activities going on. I absolutely need my morning coffee so I take a seat at the coffee/internet shop across the street and while enjoying a strong espresso, I read the Bangkok Post. The lady who owns the coffee shop is the perfect antidote for a morning mood. She's eccentric yet generous and always good-humoured. Even when I haven't been there for a while, traveling around or back home, she always welcomes me with a 'sabai dee mai, khun Tom' (How are you Mr. Tom?). Kindly, she offers me toast and some cakes to go with my coffee.

Overlooking the street, I decide to skip the western-style toast and cake and opt for 'khanom khlok', definitely one of my morning favourites and in my opinion a perfect match with a coffee.

Apart from weekends, when there are less people at the Thewet food market, and on Mondays, when they clean the pavement, there is a friendly lady preparing 'khanom khlok'.

They say that 'khanom khlok' makers are very patient and convivial people. You have to have a certain level of patience, as it takes some time to prepare.

A

Area

THEWET AREA AND THEWET FOOD MARKET
Sri Ayudhaya road, Soi 12
Chao Praya Express boat pier: Tha Thewez

For a very modest 10 Baht, considering the work she puts into it, I get five pieces of freshly baked 'khanom khlok' topped with spring onion. She hands me my breakfast in a Styrofoam container to keep it warm. Although I don't really need this as I like to eat it piping hot.

At daybreak in the Thewet area, Buddhist monks in saffron robes come out barefoot of the 'Wat Thewalat' temple to collect their alms in the neighbourhood. The lady next to the coconut puddings ('khanom khlok') who sells pork sticks ('moo yang') and grilled meatballs ('luk chin') offers some of her food to the monk. This offering goes together with a 'wai', a way of showing respect.

The 'wai' is the Thai form of greeting, like western people shake hands. You do this by putting your palms together, fingers pointing towards the sky and putting your hands close to the chest, mouth or the head and bowing your head and body slightly. The more respect you are showing or the more superior the person is you are greeting, the higher the level of your hands.

About the time when the last monks return to their temple after finishing their morning duties, Eva joins me across the street. I offer her some of my 'khanom khlok' but she hasn't got a sweet tooth. She heads for the marinated grilled pork skewers ('moo yang') next to the 'khanom khlok' lady. Along with the skewers, she orders a small ready-made plastic bag of sticky rice that is kept warm in a box. The skewers go in a separate plastic bag with some spicy chilli sauce on top.

Eva prefers a savoury dish for breakfast, which is also the case with most Thai people. Something like 'dim sum', Chinese buns ('salapao') or noodle soup as there are a few good street vendors selling this right in front of our guesthouse.

'Khlok' is the Thai word for a mortar, hence the shape of this delightful snack. In the old days it was cooked on a charcoal stove, some vendors still use the charcoal as this adds up to the taste.

ขนมครก
Coconut puddings
khanom khlok

Ingredients

- 350 ml thick coconut cream
- 50 g + 1 tbsp. sugar
- 2 and ½ tbsp. tapioca flour
- 400 g rice flour
- 50 g fresh coconut pulp, crushed finely in a mortar
- 3 tbsp. uncooked rice, crushed finely in a mortar
- 2 tsp. salt
- 750 ml light coconut milk
- 2 tbsp. vegetable oil

(Filling)

- 1 spring onion, sliced in rings or 1 cob of corn

How to make it!

Put the thick coconut cream together with 50 g of sugar into a saucepan. Allow the sugar to melt and leave to cool. When cool, add the tapioca flower. Set aside. Combine the rice flour with the crushed coconut pulp; add the ground rice, salt and 1 tablespoon of sugar. Stir and mix with the light coconut milk.

Grease in the 'khanom khlok' pan with some oil and heat on a medium gas stove. Wait a few seconds and spoon out the rice mixture with the light coconut milk until about 2/3 full. Immediately add a dab of the sweet thick coconut cream mixture over the top. Sprinkle some spring onion or some corn kernels on top. Cover it with a lid and leave to cook for a few minutes or until the pancakes are firm. Remove the cakes gently with a spoon. Clean the 'khanom khlok' pan with oil. Put two halves on top of each other and serve warm.

It's the marinade that gives the pork a tender, savoury taste. Some of the 'moo yang' vendors sell the pork cut in slices on a plate without the skewers but adding some cucumber and fresh herbs, more as an additional dish. It goes really well with the green papaya salad and some sticky rice.

หมูย่าง/หมูปิ้ง

Grilled pork

moo yang/moo ping

Ingredients (Makes 10 pieces)

- 10 wooden or bamboo skewers
- 400 g pork fillet, cut in thin strips
- 2 garlic cloves, chopped
- 6 coriander roots, scraped and chopped
- ½ tbsp. white ground pepper
- 4 tbsp. fish sauce
- 1 tbsp. light soy sauce
- 125 ml coconut cream
- 1 tbsp. vegetable oil
- 1 tbsp. castor sugar

How to make it!

Soak the skewers in water for 1 hour to prevent from burning.
Combine all the ingredients but the pork in a large mixing bowl, mix well.
Let the pork strips marinate in this mixture for at least half an hour.
'Weave' the strips of pork on the skewers and grill over charcoal for about 5 minutes, until cooked. Turn regularly.

Coriander or cilantro is very versatile. Here we are familiar with the use of stalks and leaves but in Thai cooking the root is very often used. Wash and scrape it and chop it finely. If you can't find it in your Asian supermarket, you can use the stalks of coriander instead. It won't be exactly the same thing but it's the next best option.

Chilli powder dip from the Isan

naam jim jaew

น้ำจิ้มแจ่ว

Ingredients

- 8 tbsp. lime juice
- 2 tbsp. fish sauce
- ½ tbsp. oyster sauce
- 1 tbsp. chilli powder
- 1 tbsp. toasted sticky rice, ground
- 1 shallot, sliced finely
- 2 tbsp. coriander leaves and stalks

How to make it!

Mix all the ingredients well.

Thai dim sum

khanom jeep

ขนมจีบ

If you like a small salty snack in the morning, healthy and nothing greasy, try dim sum. Just point to show which ones you want to buy.

Ingredients

- 2 dried mushrooms (e.g. cloud ear, shiitake)
- 350 g prawns, peeled, deveined and chopped
- 250 g minced pork
- 1 tsp. ginger, chopped
- 1 spring onion, chopped
- 1 shallot, chopped
- 20 wonton sheets
- 1 tbsp. oyster sauce
- 1 tsp. Chinese rice wine
- 1 tsp. sesame oil
- ½ tsp. sugar

(Dim sum sauce)

- 2 tbsp. light soy sauce
- 2 tbsp. dark soy sauce
- 1 tbsp. rice vinegar
- 1 pinch of salt
- 1 pinch of sugar

How to make it!

Soak the mushrooms in water for 15 minutes, drain and squeeze out excessive liquid. Chop finely. Combine prawns, pork, mushrooms, ginger, spring onion and shallot and mix well. Add the oyster sauce, rice wine, sesame oil and sugar and mix well. Place 2 teaspoons of this mixture in the middle of a wonton sheet. Fold sides in like shaping a goblet. If necessary, cut off excessive wonton sheet. You have to be able to see the filling. Repeat for the rest. Steam the dim sum for about 5-10 minutes (according to their filling), until cooked. In the meantime, mix all the ingredients for the sauce. Serve the dim sums with the sauce.

This is originally a Chinese breakfast. Even Thai people call it in English 'Chinese buns'. Variations of the fillings are possible. You can use red barbecued pork, black beans, etc.

When leaving a '7-Eleven'-store you might hear the employees saying ao salapao porm mai krap/ka'. Do you want anything else? Here 'anything else' is expressed by 'salapao'.

ซาลาเปา

Steamed bun

salapao

It's such a wonderful sight, all those white buns lined up in a steamer.

Ingredients (Makes 15 pieces)

- 240 ml water
- 2 tbsp. vegetable oil
- 1 tbsp. sugar
- 1 tsp. salt
- 300 g wheat flour
- ½ tbsp fresh yeast

(Filling)

- 2 tbsp. vegetable oil
- 2 shallots, chopped
- 1 spring onion, chopped
- 200 g minced pork
- 1 tsp. ginger
- 3 tbsp. soy sauce
- ½ tsp. ground white pepper
- ½ tsp. sugar
- 4 tbsp. water
- 1 tsp. sesame oil
- greaseproof paper
- 1 squirt of vinegar

How to make it!

First make the filling. Put vegetable oil in a wok, stir-fry shallot, spring onion and pork for a few minutes, until cooked. Add ginger, soy sauce, white pepper, sugar and water. Keep simmering until all the water is evaporated, and then add sesame oil. Set aside and leave for 2 hours to cool and thicken. For the dough, combine water, oil, sugar and salt in a mixing bowl. Mix thoroughly. In a larger mixing bowl, combine flour with yeast and pour in the prepared mixture. Knead until the dough is firm. Cover and leave to rise for 30 minutes at room temperature.

Divide the dough into about 15 balls. Cut greaseproof paper into 15 squares. Roll each ball flat. Add a little oil if the dough sticks too much. Scoop 1 teaspoon of the filling and place in middle of disc, fold all sides inside. Form a bun shape. Place each bun on a square of grease proof paper in a steamer. Add a squirt of vinegar to the water used for steaming; this will help to keep the buns white. Steam the buns for about 10 minutes.

ก๋วยเตี๋ยวเนื้อ

Noodle soup with beef

kuaytiaw naam nuea

Noodle soups are non-stop available and are eaten at any time of the day.

Ingredients

(Stock)

- 1 kg beef bones
- 1 beef shank
- 1 pinch of salt
- 1 pinch of sugar
- enough water to cover
- 12 crushed black peppercorns
- 2 tbsp. dark soy sauce
- 1 cinnamon stick
- 2 coriander roots, scraped and bruised
- 1 handful of coriander stalks
- 1 star anise
- 3 garlic cloves
- 1 knob of galangal, sliced
- 1 stalk of lemongrass, bruised
- 2 stalks of Chinese celery, chopped roughly
- 1 onion, quartered

(Beef balls)

- 100 g minced lean beef
- 1 large pinch of salt
- 1 large pinch of ground white pepper

(Fried garlic oil)

- 6 garlic cloves, chopped
- 60 ml peanut oil

(Bowl)

- 200 g dried rice noodles, soaked in warm water for 30 minutes
- 50 g rump of beef, sliced very finely
- 1 handful of soy bean sprouts
- 1 spring onion, chopped to garnish
- coriander leaves to garnish

How to make it!

Put all the ingredients for the stock into a large pot, bring to the boil, turn on a low heat and simmer covered for 3-4 hours, skimming regularly. Take out the shank, remove the meat from the shank and slice finely. Strain the stock and return the meat from the shank to the stock. If you have the time and want to remove all excess fat, leave the stock to cool in the refrigerator. The fat will harden on top of the stock and will be easily removed. >>

Like many dishes in Thai cuisine, an endless number of variations are possible. You can use chicken or vegetable stock, sometimes even duck broth. You can use ingredients such as fish balls, roasted red pork, wontons, chicken breast, etc.

Noodle soup carts are easy to recognise: look for a big cooking pot with different compartments: one or two with stock, one with water to blanch the noodles. You will always find a four-compartment condiment holder on the tables, chopsticks will be provided and a spoon to scoop up the soup. The four condiments are: sugar, fish sauce, roasted chilli powder and chillies in vinegar. Sometimes crushed peanuts are offered as well. Flavour the soup to your own preference.

>> Combine ingredients for the beef balls, form balls and set aside. Fry the garlic in the oil until golden and set aside. Bring the stock back to the boil. Bring a large pot of water to the boil and add the meatballs until cooked. Meanwhile, you can blanch soy bean sprouts and noodles in the same water.
A handy utensil to do this is a wire-mesh basket because you can easily 'dip' it into the water. Be careful to blanch only one small serving at a time. You can either put the raw slices of beef in your bowl or briefly blanch it in the water. Place noodles, soy bean sprouts and slices of beef in a bowl, add a few meatballs, some meat from the shank, pour over the soup. Garnish with the spring onion, coriander leaves and top with the fried garlic oil.

When Thai people say about a person that he is 'sen yai', it means that he or she is a VIP, Very Important Person.

There are two types of noodles, commonly used: rice noodles and egg noodles. Egg noodles are easy to recognise because of their yellow colour, rice noodles are white. Most noodles come in various sizes. In Thailand, rice noodles come in three sizes, usually all three available at a food stall. 'Sen yai' are wide noodles, 'sen lek' are thin noodles and 'sen mii' are very thin noodles, or rice vermicelli.

During our visits to Thailand and Vietnam, I noticed that for western visitors the breakfast of eggs, toast and coffee is a sacred thing. Everyone tried a typical Thai breakfast once, but almost never twice. Rice soup ('joak') is another traditional breakfast in Thailand. I got to know this dish when I was staying at The Atlanta hotel years ago. They still serve it over there. The hotel has an authentic lobby from the Fifties and is soaked in atmosphere.

There's a famous dessert food stall at the end of Soi Rambutri (the street parallel with Khao San Road) where I used to take our culinary tour groups to for an evening bite.
Next to this colourful orgy of sweets, tables are set out for 'joak'. The place is identifiable by the row of cooking pots with rice soup on a very long and narrow gas stove (1).

1

Address

RICE SOUP ('JOAK') FOOD STALL
Corner of Soi Rambutri and Tanao Road
in front of '7-Eleven'
Open: 18:00 – 23:00, daily

In earlier times this porridge was prepared in the evening and simmered all night on a very low heat. You can cook the rice in the stock, adding extra water or stock if necessary. Broken rice has a nuttier flavour, a firmer and stickier texture than 'whole' rice.

โจ๊ก

Rice porridge

joak

A favourite amongst Thai people, a hearty breakfast or a filling, yet digestible, late night snack.

Ingredients

- 200 g (broken) rice
- 1 l chicken stock
- 100 g minced pork
- 3 tbsp. light soy sauce
- ¼ tsp. ground white pepper
- 2 hardboiled eggs, quartered
- 2 spring onions, chopped
- 1 handful coriander leaves
- 1 tbsp. deep-fried garlic
- 1-3 large chillies
- 200 ml vinegar
- extra fish sauce

How to make it!

Rinse the rice a few times with cold water. Cook the rice using any method.
Bring stock to the boil. For extra flavour you can add Chinese celery, bruised lemongrass, cracked white peppercorns, coriander root, galangal, etc.
Add the rice and simmer briefly. Some people prefer a more porridge-like consistency, others a firmer texture of the rice. Simmer accordingly. Season it with soy sauce and pepper.
Divide eggs in bowls, scoop over the soup and finish with coriander, spring onion and garlic. Serve immediately with a small dish of chillies in vinegar, an extra bowl of fish sauce to season and accompaniments to your liking.
Other accompaniments could be fresh grated ginger, peanuts, deep-fried fish, dried shrimp or dried fish, roasted pork, raw egg yolk, stir-fried prawns, chicken, pickled vegetables, etc.

Thewet at noon

When I first met Khun Ni, she was out on the pavement with a mobile cart and plastic chairs and tables, selling various kinds of dishes to passers by. A couple of years later she was renting a house on the same street and ran a restaurant on the ground floor.

Although Khun Ni is rather shy, she always welcomes us warmly at her restaurant. The place is packed when we enter at noon. Students from the nearby college drop in for lunch. It's a pleasure to see her cook; she has that natural grace and relaxed attitude that makes it all look very simple.

Tales of Thai food vendors that started with a small cart, grew bigger and ended up as restaurant owners are endless. Occasionally some of them even own chains of restaurants. Like Ni's place, there are many, but I like her serene style and the food is good. It's a short walk from my guesthouse and there is always a positive atmosphere in her humble establishment.

A lot of different kinds of dishes are possible so the biggest problem will be what to order. It helps to have a good look at the ingredients on display in the glass showcases or on ice before ordering.

Mostly stir-fried dishes are on the menu but my personal favourite is the squid salad ('yam pla muek'). It goes well with a plate of stir-fried water spinach ('phat pak bung fai deng').

We often go to Khun Ni's restaurant if we want to have a fast lunch with no fuss. A good choice is chicken with Thai basil ('gai phat krapao') or pork stir-fried with garlic and pepper ('moo kratiem phrik thai'), served with rice of course! If desired, spice it up with fish sauce and chillies ('naam pla phrik'). This condiment is always available.

There are food stalls that specialise in making 'yam'; you will usually find them in the late afternoon as they are very spicy dishes, which is not really suitable for breakfast, and they go very will with a cold beer. In a way you could say it is drinking food.

Basically you can prepare a 'yam' with all kinds of fish, meat, even with vegetables and fruit. Two of my favourite versions are the spicy pomelo salad ('yam som oh') and the spicy crispy pork salad ('yam moo khrob'). An unexpected experience and for some a little weird is a 'yam' made out of canned mackerel. Good stuff when you go camping and lack fresh meat or fish.

'Phat fai deng' literally means: 'fried with red fire' and is probably one of the more spectacular dishes to look at while preparing. By heating the wok very high, the flame sets into the wok and gives the water spinach that smoky flavour. Some of the street vendors actually fling the water spinach into the air when the flames get into the wok and catch it again. A dangerous sight, if you ask me.

ผัดผักบุ้งไฟแดง

Stir-fried water spinach or morning glory

phat pak bung fai deng

Ingredients

- 250 g water spinach
- 1 tbsp. vegetable oil
- 2 garlic cloves, crushed
- 1 red medium chilli, sliced finely
- 2 tbsp. yellow bean sauce
- 1 tsp. sugar
- 2 tbsp. light soy sauce
- 6 tbsp. water or chicken stock

How to make it!

Put the water spinach in iced water, this will keep the water spinach nice and crispy to stir-fry. Drain. Heat the wok, add the oil and stir-fry garlic, chilli and yellow bean sauce on a medium heat. Add the water spinach; put on high heat and stir-fry until the leaves soften. Reduce the heat and add sugar, soy sauce and water or chicken stock.
Serve immediately.

ยำปลาหมึก

Squid salad

yam pla muek

Forget chewy, rubbery deep-fried squid or calamari like we get on our plates much too often. This blanched squid melts like butter and the simplicity of this dish, combined with the spicy freshness, is astonishing.

Ingredients

- 200 g fresh squid, cleaned and cut in strips or rings
- 1 sweet white onion, finely sliced
- 2 kaffir lime leaves, very finely sliced *(optional)*
- 1 stalk of lemon grass, white part sliced finely
- 10 mint leaves
- 8 coriander leaves *(optional)*
- 8 flat parsley leaves or Chinese celery leaves, shredded
- 1 small tomato, quartered
- 1 tbsp. rice vinegar

(Dressing)

- 2-4 small red and green chillies, chopped very finely
- 3 tbsp. lime juice
- 2 tbsp. fish sauce
- 1 pinch of sugar

How to make it!

Combine all the ingredients for the dressing and taste. It should taste sour, salty and spicy. Bring some salted water with vinegar to the boil and blanch the squid briefly. As soon as the squid changes from transparent to opaque, remove from the water. Put in iced water to stop the cooking process and keep aside. Gently combine the other ingredients for the salad, add the squid, pour over the dressing and serve immediately.

The squid can be replaced by other ingredients, like grilled beef, grilled prawns, crispy pork, seared tuna, etc. This is the basic recipe for a 'yam', a Thai salad. The distinctive quality about this recipe is that sweet onion is used instead of shallots. Usually, shallots are used in a 'yam' but the softer, sweet taste of the onion works very well with the delicate taste of the blanched squid.

This is one of the kicks of Thai cuisine: the sourness of the lime, combined with the spiciness of the chillies and the freshness of the herbs lift this dish up to a higher level. It's highly addictive and will make you want to beg for more!

You could also use pork instead of chicken.

ไก่ผัดใบกะเพรา

Stir-fried chicken with holy basil on rice

gai phat krapao

Ingredients

- 2 tbsp. vegetable oil
- 2 garlic cloves, crushed
- 250 g chicken breast, boned and chopped in small pieces
- 2 big red chillies, chopped finely
- 2 handful of holy basil (bai krapao)
- 2 tbsp. fish sauce
- 1 tbsp. sugar
- 2 tbsp. water or chicken stock

How to make it!

Heat the wok on a medium heat. Add oil and garlic, stir-fry for a few seconds. Turn on the heat and add the chicken. Add chilli and half of the basil. Stir-fry for 1 minute, add fish sauce, sugar and water or stock. Turn down the heat on low. Add the rest of the basil, stir-fry for a few seconds and serve on rice.

There are 3 types of Thai basil. The 2 most frequent used are Thai basil ('bai horapa') and holy basil ('bai krapao'). Bai horapa has a distinctive anise taste and is used in salads and curries. Bai krapao has a peppery flavour and is used in stir-fries. The third type is less common: lemon basil ('bai maenglak'). It has a sweet lemon taste, used in salads and soups and for adding fragrance to foods.

หมูกระเทียมพริกไทย

Stir-fried pork with garlic and black pepper

moo kratiem phrik thai

Ingredients

- 250 g pork fillet
- 1 garlic clove
- 15 white peppercorns
- 2 coriander roots, scraped and chopped
- 2 tbsp. vegetable oil
- 2 tbsp. fish sauce
- 2 tbsp. water or chicken stock
- ¼ tbsp. sugar
- 1 tsp. crushed pepper
- 1 handful coriander leaves
- 1 fried egg *(optional)*

How to make it!

Cut pork in bite-size pieces. Make a smooth paste from the garlic, white peppercorns and coriander roots, using a pestle and mortar. Heat the wok on a low heat. Add oil and stir-fry the paste for 30 seconds. Add pork and turn up the heat. Add fish sauce, water or stock and sugar and keep stirring until pork is cooked. Season this with the crushed pepper and garnish with coriander leaves.

Variations are possible with beef or prawns. When using meat, serve with steamed rice, some slices of cucumber and a fried egg, sunny-side-up on top.

This dressing is quintessentially Thai. It's the Thai equivalent of our pepper & salt, combined in one bowl. Mostly served with rice dishes but then again, a lot of dishes come with rice in Thailand.

พริกน้ำปลา

Fish sauce and chilli

phrik naam pla

Ingredients

- 3-5 medium chillies, sliced finely in rings
- 1 garlic clove, chopped finely
- 5 tbsp. fish sauce
- 1 tbsp. lime juice

How to make it!

Mix all the ingredients.

It's a common mistake that Thai food is eaten with chopsticks. Generally, it's eaten with **a spoon** (R) and **a fork** (L). Use the fork to scoop the food on your spoon and bring the spoon to your mouth. You don't need knives since everything is cut in bite-sized pieces. Only noodle soups and some noodle dishes (originating in China) are eaten with chopsticks.

Cruising on the Chao Phraya

Another great advantage of staying at Thewet is that it's near one of the stops of the Chao Phraya River Express boat. These boats run up and down the Chao Phraya River from six o'clock in the morning until seven o'clock in the evening. This is my preferred way of transportation in Bangkok. The wind offers a welcome breeze on this pleasant boat ride without traffic jams and you can enjoy the scenery, life on the river banks, the city skyline and get a glimpse of some of the major landmarks like Wat Po, Wat Arun and the Royal Palace. Whenever I'm on the boat, I am overwhelmed by an intense feeling of freedom and contentment.

The Pak Khlong Talaat (B) or Flower Market just north of the Memorial Bridge is one of my favourite stops when I go for a morning boat ride. This is one of the big wholesale markets of Bangkok. I love walking around there, soaking up the atmosphere. Just wandering around and admiring the goods on display, the quality is unbelievable. The quantity of fruits, vegetables and flowers that are sold here is mind-blowing.

I usually have a cup of hot soy milk ('naam tahuu') and some Thai donuts ('pah tong koh') after finishing my early walk.

When traveling back north on the Chao Phraya River, there's another famous food haven at hand. Behind the pier of the Siriraj Hospital (Tha Wang Lang or Siriraj Pier (C)) lies an oasis of wonderful food. Walking through the narrow lanes, it's hard to keep up with all the food hawkers and the food that's on offer. Steamed fish cake ('ha mok pla'), deep-fried spring rolls ('poh piah thod'), steamed mackerel ('pla tuu'), to name a few, all waiting to be taken away and eaten.

B

Area

PAK KHLONG TALAAT
WHOLESALE VEGETABLE MARKET
AND FLOWER MARKET
Maharat Road near Memorial Bridge
Chao Phraya Express boat pier:
Tha Rachani

C

Area

WANG LANG MARKET
Starts at 10:00 till 18:00
Next to Siriraj Hospital
Chao Phraya Express boat pier:
Tha Wang lang

A couple in love is like *pah thong koh*: An expression meaning that the parts are hard to split.

ปาท่องโก๋

Thai donuts

pah thong koh

Ingredients

- 1/4 tsp. baking soda
- 1 tsp. baking powder
- 1 tsp. sugar
- 1 pinch of salt
- 200 ml water
- 600 g flour
- 1 tbsp. vegetable oil
- oil for deep-frying

How to make it!

Mix baking soda with baking powder, sugar and salt.
Add water and flour. Stir well. Add vegetable oil and cover with a kitchen towel. Leave for 4 hours at room temperature. Heat the oil for deep-frying. Sprinkle some flour on a work surface. Take a handful of dough and make 2 rectangles (1,5cm x 6cm). Stick them together and thus forming a cross with a bit of water. Deep-fry until golden and crispy. Drain and serve.

Recently the coffee industry has boomed in Thailand. After Starbucks and the likes Thai people have picked up on the popularity of good coffee and have started to serve a real espresso, frothy cappuccino or a mellow latte. When you find a coffee stall, chances are high that a 'pah thong koh'-vendor is around.

Sometimes 'pah thong koh' is served with rice soup ('khao tom' or 'johk'). Shred it to pieces and dip it in the soup.

ห่อหมกปลา
Steamed fish cake

ho-mok-pla

Ingredients

- 1 big banana leaf, heated on a flame or blanched to make them soft and flexible
- 15 Thai basil leaves
- 175 g white fish fillet, chopped very finely
- 2 tbsp. red curry paste
- 2 tbsp. thick coconut cream
- 3 kaffir lime leaves, shredded finely
- 1 tbsp. fish sauce
- 1 egg, lightly beaten

(To garnish)

- 1 large red chilli, seeded and finely sliced in strips
- 1 kaffir lime leave, shredded very finely
- extra Thai basil leaves
- 2 tbsp. thick coconut cream

How to make it!

First, make 4 banana cups. Cut out 2 squares of 12,5 cm x 12,5 cm. Take a glass or a bowl with a diameter of 10 cm; use this as a form to cut out circles. Hold the mat or the non-glossy sides against each other; make sure the fibres are forming a cross. Make a 1 cm deep tuck 4 cm long and staple (or use wooden toothpicks). Repeat at the opposite point, then at the two side points, thus making 4 tucks. The result should be a square-shaped cup. Put some basil leaves at the bottom of the cup and set aside.

Put the fish in a mixing bowl, add curry paste, coconut cream, kaffir lime leaves and fish sauce. Combine well and mix in the beaten egg. Divide this mixture over the cup; fill maximum 2/3 of the cup. Steam the cups for 20 minutes until cooked, garnish with chilli, kaffir lime leave, basil and a bit of coconut cream and serve immediately.

This is an impressive way to serve steamed fish cake.

This is a perfect appetizer which can be made well in advance. In this recipe rice paper is used but you can also use spring roll paper. Look for it in the freezer section of your Asian supermarket. Seal it with egg white.

You can vary considerably with the fillings, to your personal taste and preference. For a more healthy variation, steam the spring rolls or, why not, opt for fresh spring rolls. Soak rice paper in warm water until soft, use fresh filling such as herbs, lettuce, cucumber, tuna, salmon, etc. Roll and... serve!

ปอเปี๊ยะทอด

Deep-fried spring rolls

poh piah thod

Originally from Chinese-Vietnamese origin but Thai people adopted this golden snack eagerly. It's now widely available in Thailand

Ingredients

- 100 g mung bean noodles
- 8 dried cloud ear mushrooms
- 200 g minced pork
- 2 garlic cloves, chopped
- 2 tbsp. fish sauce
- 2 tbsp. light soy sauce
- ½ tsp. sugar
- ½ tsp. ground white pepper
- 1 carrot, julienned
- 1 handful of soy bean sprouts
- 6 sheets of rice paper (square or round, small size)
- oil for deep-frying

How to make it!

Pour boiling water over the mung bean noodles, cover them and let this rest for 3-4 minutes. Drain well and set aside. Soak the dried mushrooms for 10 minutes in warm water and slice finely. Combine minced pork with garlic, fish sauce, soy sauce, sugar and pepper. Add mung bean noodles, mushrooms, carrot and soy bean sprouts.

Take a large bowl with warm water and put 1 rice paper in for a few seconds until soft.

Place a little bit of the mixture in the middle, fold one side over, pull back slightly and fold in the edges. Roll tightly and seal. Be careful to roll tightly to ensure all the air is removed. Heat oil in a large wok on a medium heat and deep-fry until golden brown. Drain and serve.

Once the mackerel is steamed, it's fried over charcoal until golden and eaten with a pungent dip made with shrimp paste (naam phrik kapi).

ปลาทูนึ่ง Steamed small mackerel

pla tuu neung

Ingredients

- 1 small mackerel
- 1 pinch of salt

How to make it!

Season mackerel with salt and steam for about 15 minutes until cooked.

น้ำพริกกะปิ

Shrimp paste relish

naam phrik kapi

Ingredients

- 4 garlic cloves, peeled
- 1 pinch of salt
- 1 tbsp. shrimp paste, roasted
- 4-5 small chillies
- 1 tbsp. palm sugar
- 1 tbsp. lime juice
- 1 tsp. fish sauce
- water if necessary

(To garnish)

- small egg plants
- red chillies

How to make it!

Pound garlic, salt and shrimp paste in a mortar until smooth. Add chillies. If you want a fiery dip, pound more until the chillies are pulverised. Season with palm sugar, lime juice and fish sauce. You may want to dilute it with some water. Just add spoon by spoon, the consistency should be a slightly watery paste. Garnish with red chillies and small egg plants.

Isan interlude

If you're looking for a fabulous culinary treat, hop off the boat at Tha Wang Lang and try Pa Sida's (Aunt Sida) restaurant (2). According to Aunt Sida, she has been in business for forty years. Proudly she presents us a picture of a visit by Her Majesty the Queen. This place is a Mecca of Isan (region of North-East-Thailand) food. While Pa Sida is seated between different clay and wooden mortars making tasty green papaya salads ('som tam'), the place is getting packed with students, hospital workers and passers by from the market. They all fill up on sticky rice ('khao niaw') accompanied by grilled chicken ('gai yang'), salads of minced meat ('laab') or grilled beef salad ('naam tok') and of course on her famous green papaya salad. This place has no more then eleven different kinds of papaya salad. From the more regular papaya salad with peanuts ('som tam thai') to the more extreme versions with salted black crabs ('som tam poo') and with fermented fish ('som tam pa laa'). Alternatively, I order a bamboo shoot salad ('soup nor mai').

For the food adventurous there is 'tab waan', a salad similar to 'naam tok nuea', but with liver instead of grilled beef. As there is sticky rice on the menu, this is a place where it's ok to use your hands for eating. Roll the sticky rice into a ball and dip it in or scoop up some of the food with it.

2

Address

NAMTOK SIDA
Wang Lang market
(go left along Wang Lang,
turn right in Trok Wang Lang,
next to a shop called Wienna)
Open: 09:00 – 18:00,
closed on Sundays

'Som tam' with sticky rice and grilled chicken ('gai yang') is a match made in heaven!

ส้มตำ

Green papaya salad

som tam

Ingredients

- 200 g green papaya
- 1-2 garlic cloves
- 2-5 small chilli peppers
- 1 pinch of salt
- 1-2 tsp. palm sugar
- 2 snake beans, cut in 1 cm lengths
- 2 tbsp. roasted peanuts
- 4 cherry tomatoes, halved
- 2 tbsp. dried baby shrimps
- 1 apple eggplant, sliced *(optional)*
- 2-3 tbsp. fish sauce
- 1-2 tbsp. lime juice

How to make it!

Peel and shred the green papaya. Pound the garlic with chillies, salt, and sugar in a clay mortar with a wooden pestle. Add snake beans, peanuts, tomatoes, dried shrimps and when using apple eggplant, now is the time. Keep pounding and mixing simultaneously with a large spoon. Season it with fish sauce and lime. Fold in the green papaya and continue pounding and mixing until the papaya is coated with the dressing.

This food vendor is the easiest of all to recognise. When you see a clay or wooden mortar and wooden pestle, you can be absolutely sure they are making 'som tam'. Originally a dish from the north-east, the poorer and somewhat inferior regarded Isan-region, it gained so much popularity, especially among women (no fat, good for digestion), it has become nationally widespread. Whatever its reasons or origins are, it's a fabulous, fresh and tangy delight. We just can't get enough of it!

ลาบไก่

Salad with chicken

laab gai

This is an amazing hot and sour salad, bursting with flavours but low in fat.

Ingredients

- 1 skinless chicken breast
- 1 pinch of salt
- 4 tbsp. water or chicken stock
- 2 tsp. galangal, chopped
- 1 shallot, sliced finely
- 1 spring onion, sliced in rings
- 1 tsp. chilli powder
- 5 tbsp. lime juice
- 3 tbsp. fish sauce
- 1 tbsp. sticky rice, toasted and ground
- 1 handful coriander leaves
- 1 handful mint leaves

How to make it!

Take a sharp knife or cleaver and mince chicken finely with salt. Bring water to the boil, add galangal and cook the meat until done. There should be a little bit of liquid left, if too much, discard excess liquid. Turn off the heat and add shallot, spring onion, chilli powder, lime juice and fish sauce. Check seasoning. It should taste hot and sour and then salty. Just before serving, add the toasted rice powder and finish with the fresh herbs.

This dish should be eaten with sticky rice (khao niaw) and a selection of raw vegetables such as snake beans, white cabbage, Thai basil and cucumber. Eat it with your hands: form a ball of sticky rice, dip it in the laab or use this rice ball to scoop up some of the laab.

Laab is a way of cooking; you can vary with pork ('laab moo'), beef ('laab nuea'), duck ('laab pet') or whatever you feel like eating. The preparation is basically the same but you might want to add some finely shredded kaffir lime leaves or some finely sliced lemongrass, depending on the main ingredient. For instance, kaffir lime leaves combine well when you use pork, duck or fish. If you use fish or beef, you could add lemongrass. Occasionally finely sliced snake beans or long beans are used. It's easy to experiment with this type of cooking. Try it out and see what you prefer.

If you don't want to use a whole chicken, you can prepare this recipe with drumsticks, chicken wings or chicken breast.

ไก่ย่าง

Grilled chicken

gai yang

The best version of 'gai yang' that we ate in the market in Mukdahaen, a border city in the Isan by the Mekong River.

Ingredients

- 1 small chicken (about 500 g)
- 3 coriander roots, scraped and chopped
- 10 white peppercorns
- 3 garlic cloves
- ¼ tsp. salt
- 1 stalk of lemongrass, hard bottom end cut off; outer leaves removed, white part finely chopped
- ½ tbsp. curcuma *(optional)*
- 1 tbsp. fish sauce
- 1 tbsp. sugar
- wooden sticks and iron wire *(optional)*

How to make it!

Cut chicken in half along the breastbone. Flatten out the remaining part, wash and dry. Take a pestle and mortar, pound coriander root, white peppercorns, lemongrass, garlic and salt into a fine paste. When you're using curcuma, now is the time to add it. Add fish sauce and sugar. Vigorously rub this paste into chicken, outside and inside. Marinate for 4 hours in the refrigerator.

Fix the marinated chicken between wooden sticks and secure with iron wire when using wooden sticks and iron wire. This will make it easier to turn the chicken. Chargrill chicken for about 20 minutes until cooked, turning regularly. Serve with sticky rice, sweet chilli sauce and a selection of raw vegetables.

ซุบหน่อไม้

Bamboo shoot salad

soup nor mai

Ingredients

- 1 handful bamboo shoots, julienned finely
- 1 spring onion, chopped
- 1 shallot, sliced
- 1 tsp. chilli powder
- 3 tbsp. lime juice
- 1 tbsp. fish sauce
- 1 tbsp. toasted sticky rice, ground finely
- 1 handful mint and coriander leaves

How to make it!

Bring a little bit of water to the boil. Boil the bamboo shoots for approximately 1 minute, discard most of the water. Turn off the heat. Add spring onion, shallot and chilli powder. Season it with lime juice, fish sauce and finish with toasted rice, mint and coriander.

Don't buy canned **bamboo shoots** for this recipe. Use fresh ones. Ask for it in your Thai supermarket.

Actually, 'naam tok' is related to 'laab'. The difference being that the meat is sliced and grilled instead of minced and cooked. Serve it the same way you would serve 'laab': with sticky rice and a selection of raw vegetables such as snake beans, white cabbage, Thai basil and cucumber. In Thailand this is usually prepared with beef, although sometimes pork is used. For an extraordinary experience, try this at home with fresh tuna steak!

น้ำตกเนื้อ

Grilled beef salad from Isan

naam tok nuea

'Naam tok' literally means waterfall, referring to the meat juice that forms on top of the meat as it grills. The nutty taste of toasted rice powder combined with the charcoal flavour of the meat is something to die for!

Ingredients

- 3 tbsp. lime juice
- 2-3 tbsp. fish sauce
- 1 pinch of sugar
- 1 tsp. chilli powder
- 150 g beef (tenderloin)
- 2 shallots, sliced finely lengthwise
- 1 spring onion, sliced finely in rings
- 1 stalk of lemongrass, hard bottom end cut off; outer leaves removed, white part sliced very finely in rings *(optional)*
- 1 handful of mint leaves
- toasted sticky rice, pound finely in mortar to powder

How to make it!

First make the dressing by mixing the lime juice with fish sauce, sugar and chilli powder. Balance well; this dressing should taste spicy, sour and salty.
Grill the meat, preferably on a wood charcoal grill for that authentic flavour, to your taste. Cut beef in slices (bite-size). Don't waste the meat juice, save as much as you can. Combine beef and juice with shallot, spring onion, lemongrass when using, and fresh herbs. Finish with dressing and toasted rice powder.

Thai shallots are smaller and more refined in taste than ours. If you can not find them, you can use the ones in your supermarket.

Back on the Chao Phraya

I got to know the Pa Sida restaurant thanks to our dear Thai friend, Pi Toon, who used to work in the area. She's the most amazing person and has inspired me for years. Whenever we get together, food is the main subject of our discussions. She has been a guide in the gastronomic world of Thailand and in Thai life, reflections and society. We always have so much fun discussing and eating food. One time I was using Thai to order a noodle dish in her presence called 'moo phat sii iew', she started giggling and the waitress was looking uncomfortable. Unaware of what was happening I asked for it again. As Thai language is a tonal language words have different meanings according to their tone. When the waitress was gone, I asked Pi Toon what was wrong. She explained to me that I pronounced 'sii iew' as 'sii ua' and that this means 'to come'. Well, I joked to her, I really want the dish to come!

Besides the North-South Express boat there are plenty of ferries crossing the Chao Phraya River. For a mere 3.5 Baht they will take you across from designated areas, once the ferry has filled up with enough passengers. When crossing from the Siriraj hospital to Tha Phra Chan there is the interesting Amulet market. People come from all over Thailand to buy amulets of their favourite monk.

The restaurants on the riverfront, on the right side coming from Tha Phra Chan (D) are great places to have lunch and watch life on the river pass by.

Under the shady aluminium roofs you will find a few restaurants and vendors selling crispy fried catfish ('yam pla duk foo'). This is one of my all-time favourites and an example of the yin-yang balance. The soft structure of the green sourly mango in a fresh lime and chilli dressing combined with the crispiness of the deep-fried fish and accompanied by peanuts and dried chillies, a hit!

D

Area

AMULET MARKET
Starts at 10:00 till 17:00
Maharat Road and Pra Chan Road
Chao Phraya Express boat pier:
Tha Pra Chan

This food hawker will usually also offer stir-fried noodles in gravy. It's not hard to see the similarity in the recipes.

ก๋วยเตี๋ยวผัดซีอิ๊วใส่หมู

Stir-fried noodles with pork and soy sauce

kuaytiaw phat sii iew sai moo

Ingredients

- 2 tbsp. oil
- 2 garlic cloves, crushed
- 200 g pork, cut in strips
- 1 handful wide rice noodles, soaked and drained
- 1 stalk of Chinese broccoli, cut diagonally
- 1 egg, beaten
- 1 tsp. dark soy sauce
- 2 tbsp. light soy sauce
- 1 tsp. oyster sauce
- 1 tsp. sugar
- 4 tbsp. chicken stock or water
- ¼ tsp. white pepper

How to make it!

Heat oil in a wok on a medium heat, add garlic and pork and stir-fry until coloured. Add noodles and Chinese broccoli. Stir in the egg and mix well. Add soy sauces, oyster sauce and sugar and stir-fry for another 30 seconds. Add stock or water to make a sauce. Season it with white pepper.

ก๋วยเตี๋ยวราดหน้าใส่หมู

Stir-fried noodles with pork and gravy

kuaytiaw raat na sai moo

Ingredients

- 4 tbsp. vegetable oil
- 1 handful wide rice noodles, soaked and drained
- 2 tbsp. sweet soy sauce
- 2 garlic cloves, chopped
- 100 g pork, cut in strips
- 1 stalk of Chinese broccoli, cut diagonally
- 1 handful of beansprouts
- 8 tbsp. chicken stock or water
- 1 tsp. yellow bean paste
- 2 tbsp. dark soy sauce
- 1 tbsp. light soy sauce
- 1 tbsp. tapioca flour

How to make it!

Heat 2 tablespoons of oil in a wok on a medium heat and stir-fry the noodles with the sweet soy sauce for 2 minutes. Set aside. Heat the remaining oil on a low heat and fry garlic until golden. Turn up the heat and add pork. Keep stirring until the pork changes colour. Add Chinese broccoli whilst stirring. Add stock or water, yellow bean paste, soy sauces. Stir in the tapioca flour and let the sauce thicken, like gravy. Add the noodles and combine well.

Traditionally, catfish is used to make the fish cake but it can be rather well substituted with sea bass or sea bream. Experiment with other kinds of fish to see what works as well. At the market, the three large components of this salas (fish cake, mango salad and dressing) are sold in separate bags.

ยำปลาดุกฟู

Crispy fish and green mango salad

yam pla duk foo

It's a missed opportunity that a lot of Thai restaurants abroad don't put this dish on their menus. Hard to understand because the unusual combination of textures and flavours is overly thrilling and is on the verge of perfection.

Ingredients

(Crispy fish)

- 1 catfish, sea bass, sea bream
- 1 smoked trout
- 1 large pinch of salt
- oil for deep-frying

(Dressing)

- 3 tbsp. lime juice
- 2-4 small chillies, chopped finely
- 2 tbsp. fish sauce
- 1 tbsp. sugar

(Green mango salad)

- 1 small green mango
- 2 shallots, sliced finely
- 1 handful of roasted or deep-fried peanuts
- 1 handful of mint leaves
- 1 handful of coriander leaves
- 2 deep-fried dried large chillies *(optional, for garnishing)*

How to make it!

Clean the fish (scaled, eviscerated and washed), pat dry with paper towel. Roast in the oven (190°C) on a rack until quite dry. Leave to cool. Remove bones and any hard bits. Blend with trout and salt in a food processor until the mixture is that of breadcrumbs. Pulse until the mixture has just the right texture. Too fine, and it will not cluster when it fries; too coarse, and it will harden too much. >>

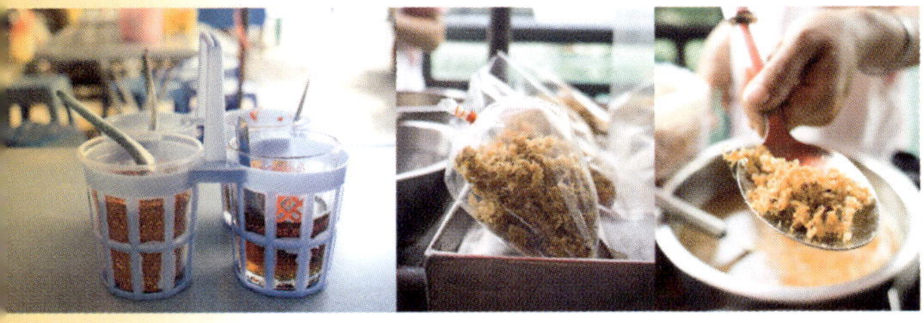

>> Bring plenty of oil in a wok to medium to high temperature. The right temperature is important. Try a first batch and adjust the heat if necessary. Too hot, the fish will burn; too cool and the collagen in the fish will not cook fast enough to hold the fish together. Deep-fry a handful at a time. After the foaming stops, mould the fish together by pushing the fish crumbs towards each other. Let the collagen do the work and you will see that it forms a cluster, a fish cake. When it smells cooked, flip over until golden in colour. Remove and drain. Give the oil some time to reheat and repeat this process.

For the dressing, combine lime juice, chillies, fish sauce and sugar.

Peel the mango and shred finely. Combine shallots, mango, peanuts, mint and coriander. Add the fish cake and the large chillies when using. Pour over dressing and serve immediately.

The restaurants on the riverfront near the amulet market offer a bit of everything. Last time Eva and I were there we spent hours talking, overlooking the river and enjoying the cooling wind. We shared a plate of grilled chicken sticks with a delicious peanut sauce ('satay gai') as a starter, followed by stir-fried broccoli with crispy fried pork belly ('phat pak kanaa') and a superbly made sour soup with prawns ('tom yam kung'). Some of my liveliest memories are food related and somehow food just tastes so much better in the company of a loved one.

Satay is always served with peanut sauce and cucumber relish. Sometimes more elaborate versions are seen, with pineapple or cherry tomato.

สะเต๊ะไก่/สะเต๊ะหมู

Grilled chicken or pork satay

satay gai / moo

Ingredients (Makes 10 pieces)

- 10 wooden or bamboo skewers
- 450 g chicken or pork fillet
- 2 tsp. coriander seeds
- ½ tsp. cumin
- 2 garlic cloves, chopped
- 4 red shallots, chopped
- 2,5 cm ginger
- 2,5 cm turmeric
- 1 tsp. salt
- 2 tbsp. vegetable oil
- 2 tbsp. fine white sugar

How to make it!

Soak the skewers in water for 1 hour; this will prevent burning while grilling. Cut the chicken or pork in fine strips. Using a pestle and mortar, pound the coriander seeds, cumin, garlic, shallot, ginger, turmeric until smooth. Add salt, oil and sugar. Let chicken or pork marinate in this mixture for at least 1 hour. 'Weave' the strips of meat on the skewers and grill, turning regularly.

Turmeric is a member of the ginger family and not, although sometimes erroneously mentioned, related to saffron. It has a tough, brown skin and is a deep orange inside. When added to foods, the orange imparts a yellow colour. This is where the confusion derives from but you can't substitute the one for the other. Turmeric has a long history of use in herbal remedies. There is a long list of ailments and diseases where turmeric can play a healing or preventing role, specifically as a powerful anti-inflammatory. It's a strong protector for your health but a messy ingredient in the kitchen. Wear gloves when you peel and chop turmeric to prevent yellow stains and fingers.

น้ำจิ้มสะเต๊ะ / น้ำจิ้มถั่ว

Peanut sauce

naam satay / naam jim thua

Ingredients

- 2 large dried chillies, chopped
- 2 garlic cloves, chopped
- 1 stalk lemongrass, chopped
- 1 tbsp. turmeric, chopped
- 2 tbsp. vegetable oil
- 450 ml coconut milk
- 1 tbsp. tamarind water
- 2 tbsp. sugar
- ½ tsp. salt
- 8 tbsp. ground roasted peanuts

How to make it!

Pound the chilli, garlic, lemongrass and turmeric in a mortar until smooth. Heat oil in a wok on a low heat and fry the paste until fragrant. Add coconut milk and bring to the boil. Keep boiling for 7 minutes. Add tamarind water, sugar, salt and peanuts. Keep on boiling for 5 minutes.

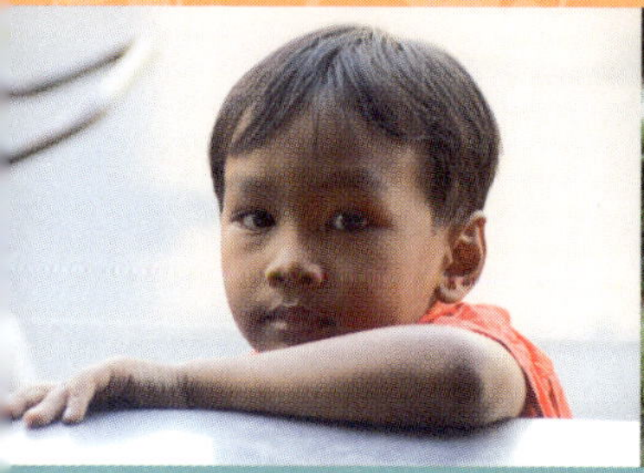

ผัดผักคะน้าหมูกรอบ

Chinese broccoli with crispy pork

phat pak kanaa moo khrob

The bitter taste of the vegetables combines magnificently with the salty, crispy taste of the pork.

Ingredients

- 1 tbsp. vegetable oil
- 1 garlic clove, crushed
- 1 small chilli, cut finely (optional)
- 2 stalks of Chinese broccoli, cut diagonally
- 2 tbsp. oyster sauce
- 1 tbsp. fish sauce
- ½ tsp. sugar
- 4 tbsp. water or light chicken stock
- 10 cm crispy pork, cut in bite-sized pieces
- ¼ tsp. freshly ground black pepper

How to make it!

Put the wok on a medium heat. When warm, add vegetable oil, garlic and chilli when using. Stir-fry for a few seconds. Add the Chinese broccoli, turn up the heat and stir-fry for 1 minute. Add oyster sauce, fish sauce and sugar, keep stir-frying for another minute. Add water or chicken stock, stir-fry for half a minute and put on a low heat. Add crispy pork and finish with pepper.

Crispy pork is used in several dishes, like noodle soups, stir-fries, but is also extraordinary in 'yam'. It adds a fantastic, salty, crispy flavour. It's easy to tell if a food stall has crispy pork, it usually hangs on display.

หมูกรอบ

Crispy pork

moo khrob

This is truly authentic Thai food, very easy to make but a little time-consuming. Start preparations well in advance.

Ingredients

- 3 tbsp. light soy sauce
- 1 pinch of salt
- 1 pinch of sugar
- 1 kg pork belly, washed
- 5 tbsp. salt
- 3 tbsp. vinegar
- oil for deep-frying

How to make it!

Mix soy sauce with a pinch of salt and sugar and marinate pork belly in the refrigerator for 2 days.

Remove from the marinade and steam pork belly for 30 minutes until cooked. Cool but do not refrigerate. Make lengthwise incisions, about ½ cm deep, be careful, only the skin, not the meat. Perforate the meat with a fork; generously rub it in with salt and vinegar.

Leave it to dry at least 1 night, preferably 48 hours. Brush off dried salt and deep-fry until pork skin has bubbled and crackled.

Drain well, cool and cut in slices.

ต้มยำกุ้ง

Hot and sour soup with prawns

tom yam kung

'Tom' means 'to boil' in Thai and 'yam' 'to mix'.

Ingredients

- 8 prawns
- 1 l water
- 1 tbsp. phrik pao paste
- 3 tbsp. lime juice
- 2-4 stalks of lemon grass, bruised
- 6 slices galangal
- 8 kaffir lime leaves, shredded
- 2 shallots, sliced
- 2 garlic cloves
- 2 tbsp. fish sauce
- 1 handful straw or oyster mushrooms, chopped roughly
- 2-4 small chillies
- 1 handful cherry tomatoes, halved
- 1 handful saw leaf herb (pak chee farang), shredded or coriander leaves, chopped
- 1 spring onion, chopped

How to make it!

Remove heads (if there) and legs of the prawns. Shell the prawns; leave shell on the tail intact. Make a small incision along the back of the prawn and remove the black intestinal tract. Keep the shells and heads for making the stock.
Bring water with shells and heads to the boil for 15 minutes. Or for a richer stock, fry the shells and heads in a bit of oil, then add water. Strain and keep the liquid.
Mix the phrik pao paste with the lime juice and set aside. >>

This soup should be eaten steaming hot. It is often served in a kind of steamboat under which burning charcoals keep this soup hot during the meal. The freshness of the ingredients is crucial to prepare a perfect 'tom yam'. By adding the lime juice at the end of the preparation, it preserves its fresh flavour. Lemon grass, galangal and kaffir lime leaves give this soup its distinctive flavour; you can find this holy threesome at most markets in Thailand, bundled together. Be careful though, you are not supposed to eat these herbs!

According to several surveys concerning the popularity of Thai food around the world, 'tom yam kung' is noted number 1 in the top 10 of favourite Thai dishes. Equally, Thai people love this spicy soup and consider this one of their national dishes.

>> Add lemon grass, galangal, kaffir lime leaves, shallots, garlic and fish sauce to the stock and bring to the boil. Add mushrooms and keep on simmering for 2 minutes. Add the prawns; once they turn pink, they are cooked. Turn of the heat. Add chilli and cherry tomatoes.

Put 1 teaspoon of the phrik pao-lime mixture in each bowl, pour over the soup and garnish with the saw leaf herb or coriander leaves and spring onion.

Whenever I catch a cold in Thailand – yes, it is possible to catch a cold in tropical weather! – I opt for 'tom yam kung'. Due to its immune-boosting ingredients it works miracles. This soup is eaten with rice; just ladle some soup over the rice. But you might want to eat it just as a soup.
Variations are possible with mixed seafood ('tom yam thaleh'), chicken ('tom yam gai') and fish ('tom yam pla').
Some cooks add (evaporated) milk or coconut milk at the end of the preparation to add a more creamy touch.

Every foreigner in Thailand is a 'farang'; it does not necessary have a pejorative association. 'Pak chee farang' literally translates as 'foreign coriander'. Also known as **saw tooth herb, long coriander, recao or culantro**. Not to be confused with cilantro, regular coriander.

Lumphini Park

Overall, Thailand is a very relaxed country. But in the streets of its capital Bangkok you will have a hard time finding a place to cool down and unwind. The traffic, the heat, the noise and the smog hit you in the face, sometimes it's just too much to handle. A great escape is Lumphini Park where you'll find thousands of people doing exercises at sunrise and sunset in a lush green area. The name, Lumphini, refers to Lord Buddha's birthplace in Nepal.

After a stroll in the park, I usually make a stop at Wireless Road in the north-east corner of Lumphini Park. There you will find one of the hidden gems of Bangkok and a gourmet food-lover's paradise. This is one of the places where eating becomes an overwhelming experience of happiness. Some might call it a culinary orgasm (3). Whenever I'm there, I never miss out on a plate of fried chicken ('gai thod'). It comes with crispy fried garlic and a sweet chilli sauce. Another must-try is the crab fried with yellow curry ('poo phat pong kari').

3

Address

KHAO TOM POLO
Corner of Wireless Road and Soi Sanam Khli
(Soi Polo 137/14), near Lumphini police station
Open: 18:00 – 22:00,
closed on Sundays

Over the years, I have recommended or invited hundreds of people to this place and every single one of them loved it. I owe this fine address to Ian, a Canadian friend and photographer, who I met in Bangkok and who still crosses our path regularly. He took us there for an unforgettable dinner party. Thanks man, you are a saint!

Because the R.B.S.C. Polo Club, part of the Royal Bangkok Sports Club, is located in the street, the two street names Soi Sanam Khli and Soi Polo are both used and known. Both are mentioned on maps and even on the street sign.

ปูผัดผงกะหรี่

Stir-fried crab with yellow curry

poo phat pong kari

Ingredients

- 250 g fresh crab meat
- 2 tbsp. vegetable oil
- 1 onion, sliced in rings
- 1 garlic clove, chopped
- 1 egg, beaten
- 2 tbsp. yellow curry powder
- 2 tbsp. soy sauce
- 1 tbsp. fish sauce
- ¼ tsp. sugar
- 2 stalks of Chinese celery, chopped roughly
- 1 handful of coriander leaves

How to make it!

Put the wok on a medium to high heat. When warm, add oil, onion and garlic and stir-fry for a few seconds. Add beaten egg and stir-fry till the egg is cooked. Add curry powder and crab and stir-fry until crab is cooked. Add soy sauce, fish sauce and sugar. Combine well. Add Chinese celery, stir and finish with fresh coriander leaves.

'Pak chee roi na' is a well known Thai saying that means 'to top it with coriander'. It's used for cover-ups or when things are made to look better than they are.

ไก่ทอด
Deep-fried chicken
gai thod

Sprinkle, Soi Polo-style, some deep-fried garlic on top.

Ingredients

- 4 garlic cloves, chopped
- 4 coriander roots, chopped
- 10 white peppercorns
- 4 tbsp. flour
- 1 egg, lightly beaten
- 2 tbsp. water
- 2 tbsp. fish sauce
- 2 tbsp. light soy sauce
- 8 chicken legs or drumsticks
- oil for deep-frying
- sweet chilli sauce for serving

How to make it!

Pound the garlic, coriander root and white peppercorns in a mortar until smooth. Mix flour with beaten egg, water, fish sauce and soy sauce. Dip chicken in batter and deep-fry until golden and crisp. Serve with sweet chilli sauce.

น้ำจิ้มไก่ย่าง

Sweet chilli dip

naam jim gai yang

The Thai name is somewhat misleading, as it literally means 'dip for grilled chicken'. No worries, it can be served with plenty of other dishes..

Ingredients

- 7 large, red chillies, deseeded and chopped
- 2 garlic cloves, chopped
- 12 tbsp. vinegar
- 8 tbsp. sugar
- ½ tsp. salt

How to make it!

Pound the chillies and garlic in a mortar until smooth. Bring vinegar, sugar and salt to the boil. Stir until sugar has dissolved. Turn down the heat to medium. Add chilli paste and simmer until it has a syrup-like consistency.

Saochingcha area

The Saochingcha area (E), located between Tanao Road and the Bangkok City Hall, used to be a Chinese trading area. Nowadays, it is packed with well-known street food vendors and restaurants. To name a few, there is 'Raat Na Yod Pak' (4) on Tanao Road where they serve excellent rice noodles and pork gravy ('raat na'). A little further down, there's 'Gai Yang Boran' (5), where grilled chicken ('gai yang') is the main attraction. One of my preferred places in this part of town is 'Chote Chitr' (6). Here you will find traditional Thai food, an all-time favourite of many food lovers. It's just off Tanao Road in a pleasantly quiet area. Signature dishes are the crispy fried noodle salad ('mee khrob'), served with a sour fruit called 'som sa' and the banana flower salad ('yam hua pli').

'Chote Chitr' opened its door ninety years ago as a herbal medical shop since the first owner Khun Chote was a traditional Thai medicine doctor. His wife, who had worked at the royal kitchens, started to serve food filled with herbs and spices for healing benefits. Today still you can sample the 'kaeng liang', more a hearty soup then a curry. It's filled with the freshest vegetables and herbs and infused with black pepper. According to my Thai friend Pi Toon 'kaeng liang' is traditionally, but not exclusively, eaten by breastfeeding women for its nutritious qualities. Recent research at the Institution of Nutrition, Mahidol University Bangkok, indicates that 'kaeng liang' can help prevent colon cancer. Further research will be conducted to investigate the benefits.

Chote Chitr is a great place to have a healthy meal after you enjoyed an invigorating massage at Wat Pho, at walking distance.

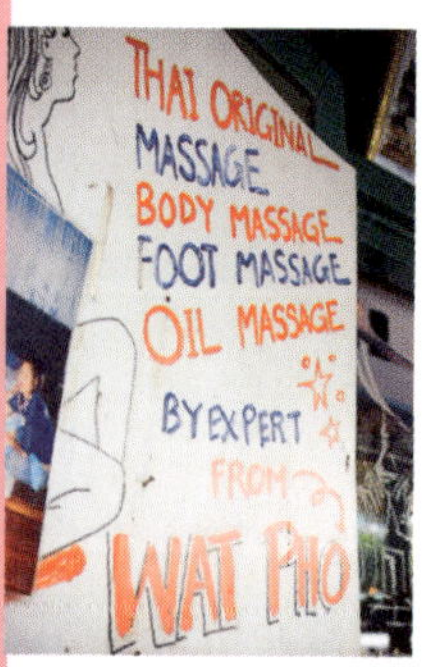

E

Area

SOACHINGCHA
Along Tanao Road and Dinso Road

4

Address

RAAT NA YOD PAK
Tanao Road, on right side between Thanon Phreang Sanphasat and Thanon Phreang Nara
Open: 09:00 – 21:00, daily

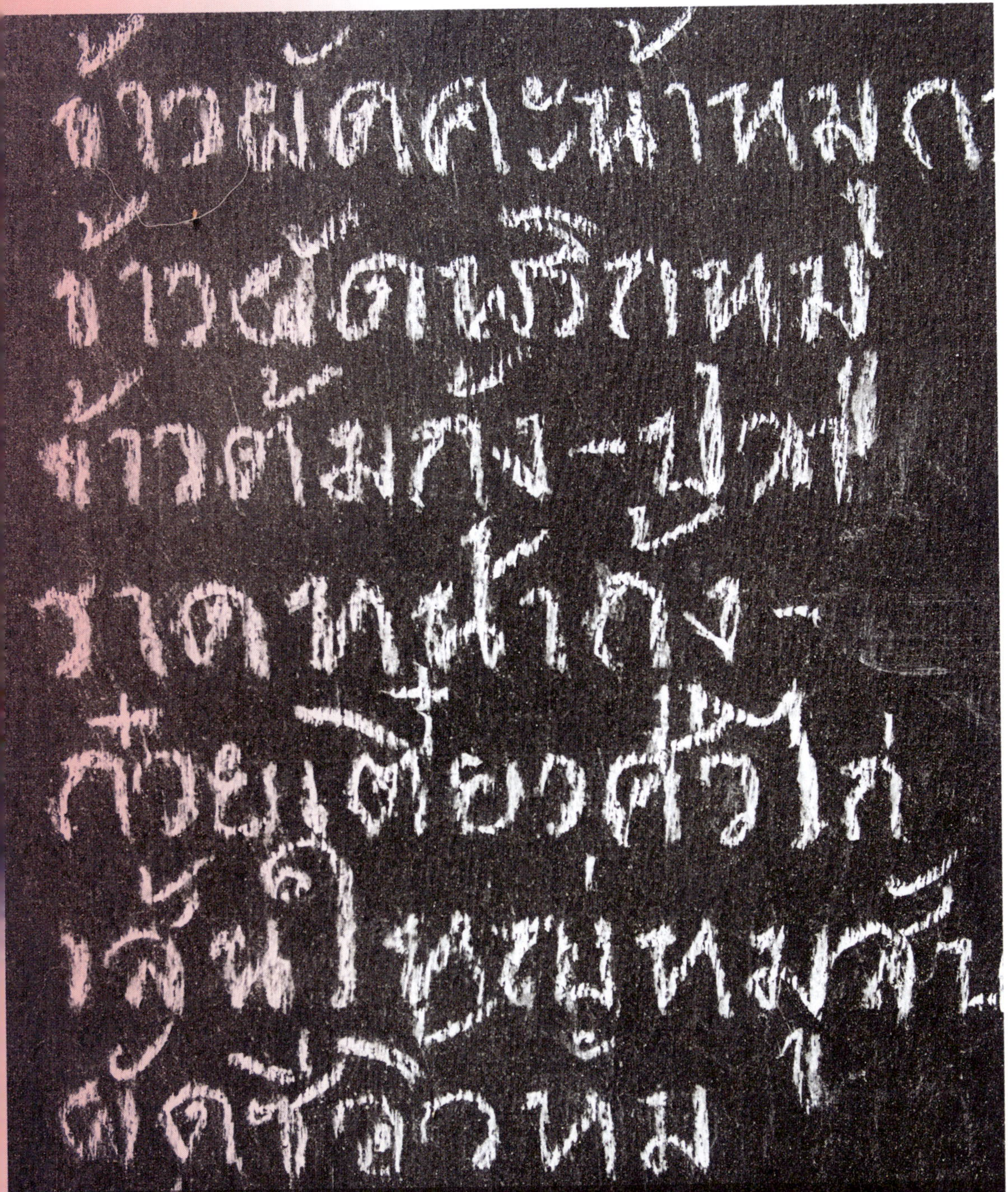

5

Address

GAI YANG BORAN
474-476, Tanao Road
Open: 09:00 – 20:00, daily

6

Address

CHOTE CHITR
146, Prang Pu Thorn, off Tanao Road
Open: 11:00 – 23:00,
closed on Sundays

'Liang' means 'at hand' or grown nearby, referring to the fresh ingredients used in this curry-like soup.

แกงเลียง

Vegetable soup

kaeng liang

Most herbs and vegetables are hard if not impossible to get your hands on outside Asia, so we suggest some alternatives.

Ingredients

(Paste)

- 1 tsp. black peppercorns
- 4 tbsp. finger root or krachai, chopped
- 1 tbsp. garlic cloves, chopped
- 4 tbsp. shallot, chopped
- 4 small chillies, chopped
- 12 tbsp. oyster or straw mushrooms, chopped
- 1 and ½ tbsp. salted bean paste

(Soup)

- 1 l water or chicken stock or vegetable stock
- 1 pinch of salt
- 8 tbsp. Thai or Japanese pumpkin, cut in bite-sized pieces
- 16 tbsp. of young bottle gourd or 1 small cucumber, cut in bit-sized pieces
- 16 tbsp. of angle loofah or 1 small zucchini, cut in bite-sized pieces
- 12 prawns, shelled and deveined (optional)
- 1 tsp. light soy sauce
- 1 pinch of palm sugar
- 1 handful of ivy gourd or young spinach
- 1 handful of lemon basil

How to make it!

Pound the ingredients for the paste gradually in a mortar using a pestle until smooth. Bring water or stock and salt to the boil and add paste. Stir well. Add pumpkin, gourd or cucumber, angle loofah or zucchini and simmer until soft. When using prawns, this is the time to add them. Add soy sauce and palm sugar and mix. Add ivy gourd or young spinach and lemon basil and serve immediately.

Finger root is named for its hand and finger-like appearance. It's also known as 'lesser ginger' and 'lesser galangal'. Besides the use in herbal medicine, finger root is commonly used in Thai cooking. It has a sharp and spicy flavour and would benefit the digestion process. If you can't find fresh finger root, look for it in the freezer section of your Asian supermarket.

ยำหัวปลี

Banana flower and chicken salad

yam hua pli

Ingredients

- 1 banana flower
- 1 tbsp. lime juice
- water
- 200 g chicken breast
- 200 ml coconut cream
- 1 tbsp. roasted chilli paste
- 1 tbsp. fish sauce
- 1 tsp. sugar
- 3 tbsp. lime juice
- 1 stalk of lemon grass, white part sliced finely
- deep-fried cashew nuts *(optional)*
- 1 handful of coriander leaves
- 2 kaffir lime leave, shredded very finely
- 2 small red chillies, deep-fried

How to make it!

Remove the outer leaves of the banana flower. Quarter lengthwise and remove the core. Slice very finely and leave to soak for at least an hour in a mixture of water and lime juice to reduce the bitter flavour. Boil the chicken in the coconut cream for about 10 minutes on a low heat until cooked. Take out the chicken and keep the coconut cream to make the dressing. Cut chicken in fine slices. Combine coconut cream with chilli paste, fish sauce, sugar and lime juice. Mix the drained banana flower, lemon grass, cashew nuts, if using and chicken and mingle all this with the dressing. Garnish with the coriander, kaffir lime leaves and chilli.

Select only firm and fresh looking **banana flowers**. It's also known as 'banana blossom' and 'banana heart'. If you can't find this in your Asian supermarket, you can substitute it with Belgian endives.

หมี่กรอบ

Crispy noodles

mee khrob

There are countless recipes for crispy noodles. Basically, it's deep-fried rice noodles, coated with a thick, sweet dressing.

Ingredients
- 100 g dried thin rice noodles
- 1 egg, lightly beaten
- 1 handful of soybean sprouts
- 1 big, red chilli, in julienne
- 1 handful of Chinese chives, chopped
- 1 handful of coriander leaves
- oil for deep-frying
- 1 tbsp. orange zest, grated

(Sauce)
- 2 coriander roots, scraped and chopped
- 4 garlic cloves
- 10 white peppercorns
- 1 pinch of salt
- 2 tbsp. vegetable oil
- 200 ml yellow bean paste
- 200 g sugar
- 2 eggs, lightly beaten
- 100 ml lime juice
- 3 tbsp. orange juice

How to make it!

Soak the noodles in water for 10 minutes, drain and mix with beaten egg. Leave to dry for at least 2 hours or preferably overnight.

Pound the coriander root together with the garlic, white peppercorns and salt until smooth. Fry this paste on a low heat in oil until golden, add yellow bean paste and sugar. Once the sugar is dissolved, add the eggs. Keep stirring. Simmer until thick, and then add lime and orange juice. Simmer for a few more seconds and turn down the heat. Leave to cool.

Heat enough oil on a medium to high heat. Deep-fry the noodles in a few batches. The noodles will puff up and change colour, turn and remove with a strainer. Drain on a paper towel. Reheat the sauce carefully on a low heat, add the crispy noodles. Make sure the noodles are evenly coated with the sauce. Gently mix with the soybean sprouts, chilli, Chinese chives and grated orange zest.

In Thailand a fruit, called 'som sa' is used instead of an orange. It tastes slightly more bittersweet, but orange or tangerine as a substitute can be used equally well.

Chinese chives: a member of the onion family, the taste is more reminiscent of garlic than onion. If not available, substitute it with regular chives and some chopped garlic.

Sweet stuff

After a meal at Chote Chitr, I never fail to stop around the corner for dessert, though it's more a snack than a dessert. On Tanao Road you will find 'Kao Niaw Korpanich' (7). This 75 year old place specialises in sticky rice with mango. Look for the many mango sellers in front of the shop. If you're looking for a place to sample the ultimate sticky rice with mango ('khao niaw mamuang'), this is the one to go for. The secret lies in the high quality of the ingredients and the cooking to perfection.

The mango sellers in front of the shop have different varieties on offer. You can find here the 'oak wrong' variety, which is sweet and juicy. It's the most expensive one. Other varieties are the 'nam dokmai', less juicy and more firm but still sweet or the 'tong dam' variety which has a more sourly taste.

7

Address

KAO NIAW KOR PANICH
431-433, Tanao Road
Open: 6:30 – 19:30,
June through December: closed on Sundays

ข้าวเหนียว
Sticky rice

khao niaw

When you see a bamboo basket placed on a pot, you can be sure it's sticky rice.

Ingredients

- sticky rice
- water

How to make it!

Rinse sticky rice frequently until the water is clear. Leave the sticky rice soak for one night in cold water. If you don't have that much time, settle for at least 3 hours in warm water. Steam the sticky rice in a bamboo steam basket for 20 minutes. Cover with a lid or a kitchen towel. Turn regularly so that the rice can steam equally.

ข้าวเหนียวมะม่วง

Sweet sticky rice with coconut and mango

khao niaw mamuang

A must-try! This combination is awesome. Use Thai mangos, irreplaceable in this recipe.

Ingredients

- 400 g sticky rice
- water for steaming
- 400 ml coconut milk
- 125 g sugar
- 1 tsp. salt
- 1 pandan leave (optional)
- 1 or 2 ripe mangos
- roasted sesame seeds (optional)

How to make it!

Steam the sticky rice according to the recipe above. Put the coconut milk in a pan on a low heat. Add sugar, salt and pandan leave when using and let simmer gently for 10 minutes. Remove the pandan leave and wring it above the coconut milk. Pour half of this mixture over the warm sticky rice. The sticky rice has to be moist but not drowned in coconut milk. Leave to stand for 15 minutes.
Peel the mango and cut in small cubes. Put the sticky rice in small serving bowls, spoon over a few tablespoons of the other half of the (warm) coconut mixture and scoop some mango cubes on top. Sprinkle with some sesame seeds.
The perfect afternoon snack before heading towards the Grand Palace and Wat Pho!

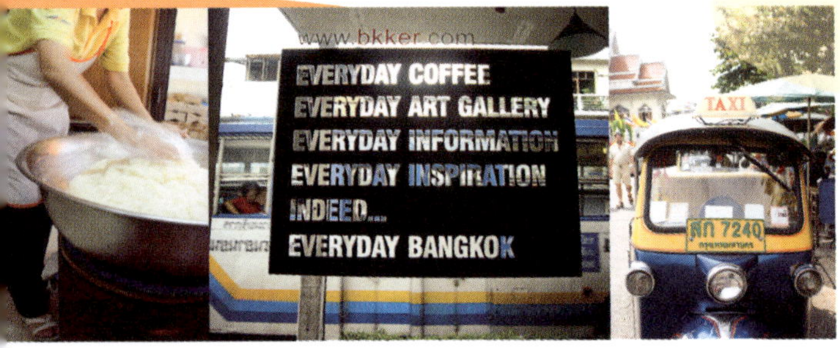

Pandan leaves are used in Thai cooking for their distinctive flavour but also in the Thai bathroom to add an essence to the water used for washing. You could say it's the vanilla of the Thai cuisine. You may even find the pandan odour in cars or taxi's. Thanks to its medicinal qualities, it keeps the heart and liver in good condition, relieves fever and soothes a sore throat.

8

Address

MON NOM SOD 1
160/2-3, Dinso Road
Open: 14:00 – 24:00, daily

On the subject of desserts and sweets, in the same area just across from the Bangkok City Hall you can find a typical Thai dessert that we westerners may frown upon, because it's such a common thing for westerners to eat. I'm talking about toast. It's widely popular and it isn't perceived as weird at all by Thai people. I guess white bread is as exotic for Thai people as curries are for us.

'Mon Nom Sod' (8) was opened in the beginning of the Eighties and it hasn't lost any of its attraction since. Every moment they're open, the place is packed. And if you don't leave fast enough after you've had your toast, the staff will give you the evil eye. It's a hip hangout among Thai teens, who gather there sipping milk straight from the farm and nibbling their toast with topping. Contrary to general beliefs, teens in Thailand like to hang out in a smoke- and alcohol-free atmosphere. Popular choices are toast with Thai custard cream or butter, jam, chocolate spread, condensed milk with sugar, cheese or honey.

Still on the sweet tour, you can find a most wonderful air-conditioned shopping mall 'The Old Siam Plaza' (F) just north from the Indian market of Pahurat and a 15-minute walk south of the Saochingcha area. This place is surely an inspiration for every pastry chef on the planet. On the ground floor of one of the oldest shopping malls in Bangkok, you can watch the food vendors carefully prepare their delicate and sophisticated snacks. It's mostly sweets that are on offer, some of them originating from the sophisticated royal Thai cuisine. There's no place to take a seat, so it's mainly take-away.

F

Area

OLD SIAM PLAZA
Burapha Road, Phranakorn, near Little India
Open: from 09:00 – 21:00

You can find a few authentic 'khanom buang' sellers in the Banglampoo area.

There is 'Khanom Buang' (9) where you can either eat them slightly warm at the shop or take them home in a nice box. It's a perfect take-away candy or after dinner sweet to surprise your friends at a home cooking party.

Also famous is 'Khanom Buang Phraeng Nara' (10), which is located on Tanao Road, a hole in the wall on the right side if you walk down from Ratchadamnoen Avenue.

This owner used to work for the Thai Railway Company before becoming a dedicated 'khanom buang'-maker. It is exported to many countries abroad.

9

Address

KHANOM BUANG
100-102, Phra Sumen Road, on your right side, coming from the fort, halfway between Phra Athit Road and Samsen Road
Open: 09:00 – 18:00, closed on Sundays

10

Address

KHANOM BUANG PHRAENG NARA
Tanao Road, on your right side, walking down from Ratchadamnoen Avenue
Open: 10:00 – 18:00, closed on Sundays

Pumpkin with custard สังขยาฟักทอง

sang khaya phak tong

Ingredients

- 1 small Japanese pumpkin
- 8 eggs, lightly beaten
- 16 tbsp. coconut cream
- 8 tbsp. palm sugar
- 1 pinch of salt
- 4 pandan leaves, shredded

How to make it!

Wash and dry the pumpkin. Take a sharp knife, cut off the top of the pumpkin so you form a kind of lid. Scoop out all the seeds. Mix the eggs with the coconut cream, palm sugar and salt. Whisk until the sugar has dissolved. Add the shredded pandan leaves. Pour this mixture in the pumpkin using a strainer. Steam the pumpkin for about 30-40 minutes, depending on the size of your pumpkin. Leave to cool at room temperature and divide into parts.

ฝอยทอง
Golden threads
foi tong

'Tong' means gold and that is exactly the colour of these tiny precious sweets.

Ingredients
- 12 yolks, preferably from duck eggs
- 1 kg castor fine sugar
- 1,5 l water

How to make it!
Strain the yolks through a very fine sieve or damp muslin. Leave this mixture overnight in the refrigerator. Warm water in a pan and dissolve the sugar. Turn on the heat until this syrup starts to boil. For the next step, you need a funnel with as small an opening as you can find. Or use an icing bag with the finest nozzle. Pour a few tablespoons of the mixture into the funnel or icing bag. Stream in a circular motion about 10 cm above the bubbling part of the syrup. Turn the heat down to medium. Cook for about 1 minute. Turn heat to very low. Using a large chopstick, collect the strands and pull them out of the syrup. Place and fold on a plate to cool. The cooking process should take no more than 30 seconds.

ขนมเบื้อง

Crispy coconut pancakes with salty or sweet topping

khanom buang

Ingredients

(Dough)

- 500 ml water
- 4 tbsp. cocoa powder (e.g. Ovaltine, Milo)
- 500 g toasted yellow bean powder
- 1 kg rice flour
- 6 eggs
- 700 g sugar

(Filling)

- 15 eggs, only the egg white
- 2 kg coconut sugar

(Topping)

Sweet

- golden threads (see recipe on previous page)

Savoury

- 5 coriander roots, scraped and chopped
- 50 g white peppercorns
- 500 ml water
- 24 tbsp. sugar
- 300 g fresh prawns, minced
- 1 tsp. salt
- 3 fresh coconuts, flesh shredded
- red or orange food colouring

(Garnish)

- shredded fresh coconut
- toasted sesame seeds
- fresh coriander leaves

>>

As you can tell by the recipe this is a very elaborate procedure and difficult to make it. In fact, there is a proverb in Thailand that says, literally translated, 'don't make khanom buang with your mouth', meaning 'if you don't know how to do it, don't do it'.

How to make it!

For the dough, mix the cocoa powder with water. Add yellow bean flour and rice flour. Knead until dough doesn't stick. Mix in eggs thoroughly. Add sugar and knead until the sugar has dissolved completely.

For the filling: take a clean, fat-free bowl. Put your mixer on medium-high speed and mix the egg whites until you see soft peaks. Gradually add the coconut sugar and keep mixing until sugar has dissolved. Stiff peaks are the sought after result.

For the savoury topping: pound the coriander root with the peppercorns, using a pestle and mortar, until smooth. Heat water and sugar in a large pan on a medium heat, stir in the paste. Add prawns, salt, fresh coconut and food colouring. Stir until the water has evaporated. Set aside.

For a savoury 'khanom buang': put a hotplate on medium heat. Carefully spread a thin layer, forming a little pancake. Cover with a thin layer of the filling. Dab some of the savoury topping on it and garnish with shredded coconut, sesame seeds and coriander leaves. Fold the pancake in half while removing it with a spatula.

For a sweet 'khanom buang': put a hotplate on medium heat. Carefully spread a thin layer, forming a little pancake. Cover with a thin layer of the filling. Dab some of the sweet topping on it and garnish with shredded coconut and sesame seeds. Fold the pancake in half while removing it with a spatula.

A 'khanom buang' maker is a skilled worker; it takes a fine technique and perfect timing to form the crispy pancakes. They come in two varieties. The sweet yellow one with golden threads ('foi tong') and the savoury orange one made with shrimp and coriander. These pancakes should be very crispy. Don't be tempted by the inferior whipped cream version that you can find at most food markets.

Chinese influence

One of the main influences in Thai cuisine is Chinese. Chinese immigrants have been working here since the founding of Bangkok. The area of the Royal Palace used to be the Chinese quarter. They were forced to relocate south to Yawalat Road when the palace was built and Bangkok became the capital. I love wandering around in Bangkok's Chinatown, a micro-cosmos, where the temples and the languages are different. And, where the food is different as well, like the expensive bird nest soup ('rung nok') and shark's fin soup ('hoo pla chalon').

A perfect example of a Chinese dish that is available from Hong Kong to Singapore is chicken on rice ('khao man gai'). 'Gai ton Pratunam' (11) has a solid reputation as being one of the best places in Bangkok to sample this dish, although there are many places around that sell it. Look for boiled chickens, hanging in glass showcases.

A similar version is prepared with duck ('khao na pet'). So duck lovers, head to 'Pet Tun Jao' (12). They sell around sixty ducks a day in many different dishes.

11

Address

GAI TON PRATUNAM
30, Petchaburi Road Soi,
opposite Pratunam Plaza, Pratunam
Open: 18:00 – 2:00, daily

12

Address

PET TUN JAO
945, Soi Wanit 2,
near the Harbour Department building
Open: 10:30 – 17:00,
closed on Sundays

Originally a specialty from the Chinese island of Hainan brought to Thailand with the many poor Chinese immigrants. They had to be inventive and economical. Therefore, nothing is wasted. The chicken legs are deep-fried. The carcass and neck are used to make a stock. The stock serves as liquid to cook the rice, to eat as a soup and is used in the accompanied sauce.

ข้าวมันไก่

Chicken on rice

khao man gai

It's easy to spot the boiled chickens hanging on a hook on display accompanied by a large rice pot. This dish smells delicious and the fragrant rice is astonishing. Most Thai dishes are shared but this is more a 'one person - one plate' example. The soup served with this dish is heartwarming and makes this a complete meal.

Ingredients

- 1 whole chicken
- 4 l water
- 1 pinch of salt
- 1 pinch of pepper
- 8 garlic cloves
- 2 coriander roots, scraped and bruised
- 1 handful of coriander stalks
- 500 g rice
- 100 g sticky rice, soaked in warm water for at least 3 hours
- 4 tbsp. vegetable oil
- 1 pinch of salt
- 1 pinch of sugar

(Soup)

- 1 small green gourd, peeled, deseeded and diced
- 1 tbsp. light soy sauce
- 1 pinch of white pepper
- 1 tbsp. spring onion, chopped
- 1 tbsp. coriander leaves

(Sauce)

- 4 tbsp. chicken stock
- 4 tbsp. yellow bean paste
- 1 tbsp. dark soy sauce
- 1 tbsp. ginger, chopped
- 1 tsp. sugar

(For garnish)

- ½ cucumber, sliced
- coriander leaves

How to make it!

Wash and clean the chicken. Put it in a large pot, cover with water; add salt, pepper, 3 garlic cloves, coriander roots and stalks, turn on a low heat and simmer for 30 minutes, skimming regularly. Turn off the heat and leave the chicken in the stock to cool. Remove the chicken, take off the skin and remove the bones. Keep the meat separate. Skim off excess fat and strain. Chop the rest of the garlic finely and set aside. >>

This type of hawker often also sells red pork on rice ('khao moo deng').

>> Combine the 2 types of rice, rinse well and drain. Heat oil in a large pot on medium heat, add garlic and fry until golden. Take out 1 teaspoon of the fried garlic and set aside on a paper towel. Add rice and keep stirring for a few minutes. Season this with salt and sugar. Ladle enough stock over the rice to cover it.

Most Thai people don't measure rice and water; they just take enough water so that the water covering the rice is in between the first and the second joint of your index finger. Do the same with the stock. Stir well, cover with a lid and cook over a very low heat until the rice is cooked. This should take about 20 minutes. Add extra stock if needed.
Bring the remaining stock back to the boil, add the green gourd and simmer for about 10 minutes. Add soy sauce, pepper, spring onion, coriander and the reserved fried garlic. Combine all the ingredients for the sauce and mix well.

Spoon some of the rice on a plate, slice the meat of chicken and put it on top. Garnish with cucumber and coriander leaves. Serve with a bowl of soup and a small dish of sauce.

หมูแดง

Red pork

moo deng

In every Chinatown in the world, you will see this red pork on offer. Originally Chinese, you can tell by the use of five-spice powder, this delicacy has found a firm place in the Thai kitchen.

Ingredients

- 1 pork tenderloin
- 1 tbsp. fish sauce
- 1 tbsp. dark soy sauce
- 1 tbsp. sugar
- 1 tbsp. ginger, chopped
- ½ tbsp. sesame oil
- ½ tsp. red food colouring
- 1 tsp. five-spice powder

How to make it!

First make the marinade. Mix all the ingredients except for the pork. Marinate the pork in this mixture for at least 3 hours in the refrigerator. Remove from the marinade and sear the pork on all sides over a charcoal grill. Turn regularly and baste with leftover marinade until cooked (about 15 minutes). Leave to cool. Cut in very thin slices.

Straight from the sea

My favourite time for visiting Chinatown (G) is at night time, when Yawalat Road is lit by the Chinese neon lights and the streets are packed with people cooking and eating. Woks are burning red, the smell of garlic in the air, people queuing up at their desired food stall. It's not an uncommon sight to see a brand new Mercedes parked here, the owner waiting to be served a 20 Baht noodle soup from a street food vendor. One of the great luxuries of Chinatown is the abundance of seafood: prawns, scallops, oysters, fresh fish, crabs, mussels, etc. We hardly ever get that quality back home and surely never at that price.

For some real Thai food ambiance in a colourful setting just ask for Soi Texas in Chinatown. Look out for the green polo t-shirts, that's T & K Seafood (13). These guys do wonderful seafood. Prices are very reasonable and the taste is as fresh as it can be. You might have to queue up if you want a table outside but it usually doesn't take very long before you will be seated.

Huge barbecued prawns come with a spicy seafood dip ('naam jim thaleh'). The deep-fried crab ('poo jaa'), presented in its shell and the clams stir-fried in chilli paste and Thai basil ('hoi laai phat phrik pao') are two other dishes definitely worth checking out. Try also the steamed sea bass with lime dressing ('pla ka pong nung manao'); if you're fond of healthy spicy-sour dishes, you will love it.

G

Area

CHINATOWN
Yawalat Road and side roads
Starts around 18:00 till midnight

13

Address

T & K SEAFOOD
49-51, Phadung Dao Road (Soi Texas), corner of Yawalat Road and Soi Texas
Open: 16:30 – 24:00, daily

NAM SING
BIRD NEST
SHARK FINS
SEA FOOD
369
T&K SEAFOOD
PRAWN
CRAB
SPAWN CRAB
SEA FISH
SQUID
SNAIL
COCKLE
MUSSLE
OYSTER
TOMYAM SOUP
FRIED VEGETABLE
FRIED OYSTER
SHARK FINS
BIRD NEST
T & K
SEAFOOD
OLD SHOP ORIGINAL YAOWARAJ
300

น้ำจิ้มทะเล

Spicy seafood dip

naam jim thaleh

Ingredients

- 5 garlic cloves, chopped
- 4-6 small green chillies, chopped
- 5 tbsp. lime juice
- 4 tbsp. fish sauce
- 1 tsp. sugar
- 2 tbsp. coriander leaves, chopped *(optional)*

How to make it!

Pound the garlic and chillies in a mortar until smooth. Add lime juice, fish sauce and sugar and mix well until sugar has dissolved. Add coriander leaves when using.

Deep-fried crab ปูจ๋า

poo jaa

Ingredients

- 400 g crab meat or 6 fresh small crabs
- 2 garlic cloves, chopped
- 1 tbsp. coriander leaves, chopped
- 1 pinch of ground black pepper
- 200 g minced pork (or chicken to substitute)
- 1 shallot, chopped
- 1 stalk of spring onion, chopped
- 2 tbsp. fish sauce
- 1 tsp. sugar
- 2 eggs, lightly beaten
- 6 crab shells if using crab meat

(For garnish)

- coriander leaves, chopped
- 1 large red chilli, julienned

How to make it!

When you're using fresh crabs, boil shortly in salted water until cooked. The cooking time depends on the size of the crabs. Ask your fishmonger how long they need to be cooked. Remove the meat and keep the shells. Clean the shells. Combine garlic, coriander and pepper in a mixing bowl. Add pork, crabmeat, shallot, spring onion, fish sauce and sugar. Mix well. Divide the mixture over the shells. Steam this for about 15 minutes. Set aside to cool. Dip the steamed crab in the beaten eggs. Deep-fry on a medium heat, meat side down, until golden. Be careful not to deep-fry too long or the filling will fall out. Remove and drain well. Garnish with coriander leaves and chilli. Serve with cucumber relish ('ar jard') or with sweet chilli dip ('naam jim gai yang').

Sometimes the fish is half-steamed served in a bowl, shaped like a fish. Under this tray are burning charcoals so the fish can steam further when already served on the table.

ปลากะพงขาวนึ่งมะนาว

Steamed sea bass with lime dressing

pla ka pong neung manao

This is Eva's favourite! The fresh taste of the fish, the spicy-sour dressing, it all combines into a perfect, pure dish. And it's so easy to make it!

Ingredients

- 1 whole sea bass or 400 g white fish fillet
- 2 stalks of lemon grass, bruised
- 4 kaffir lime leaves
- 6 slices galangal
- 1 coriander root, scraped and bruised
- 1 pinch of salt

(Dressing)

- 2 tbsp. coriander root, chopped
- 2 tbsp. garlic cloves, chopped
- 1 large red chilli, deseeded and chopped finely
- 5–20 small chillies, chopped
- 3 tbsp. fish sauce
- 4 tbsp. lime juice
- 1 tbsp. sugar
- 1 pinch of salt

(For garnish)

- 1 lime, sliced thinly
- 1 Chinese celery, chopped

How to make it!

Put lemon grass, kaffir lime leaves, galangal and coriander root scattered on a plate. Put the fish on top and season with some salt.
Steam this for about 15 minutes, depending on the size of the fish until cooked. Combine all ingredients for the dressing and mix well.
When the fish is cooked, place the fish on a serving plate, scoop over some of the cooking liquid. Pour over the dressing, garnish with a few slices of lime and Chinese celery and serve immediately.

หอยลายผัดพริกเผา

Clams with roasted chilli paste

hoi laai phat phrik pao

Ingredients

- 300 g fresh clams, soaked in salted water for a few hours to discard sand
- 2 tbsp. vegetable oil
- 2 garlic cloves, chopped finely
- 1 tbsp. fish sauce
- 1 tsp. sugar
- 2 tbsp. roasted chilli paste
- 1 large red chilli, sliced diagonally
- 2 handful of Thai basil

How to make it!

Put the wok on a medium to high heat. When warm, add oil. Add garlic and clams. Stir-fry till the clams open. Add fish sauce, sugar and chilli paste and stir. Add chilli and Thai basil and stir.

'Phrik pao' works amazingly well with seafood of any kind. Sometimes it's used as a dip sauce. It is essential in a 'tom yam kung'.

น้ำพริกเผา

Chilli paste

naam phrik pao

The 'magic sauce' according to our dear friend Pi Toon and we can only, as always, agree with her.

Ingredients

- oil for deep-frying
- 15 shallots, sliced
- 8 garlic cloves, sliced
- 8 tbsp. dried shrimp, rinsed and dried
- 8 tbsp. dried large red chillies, deseeded and chopped
- 10 slices galangal
- 1 tsp. shrimp paste, roasted
- 10 tbsp. palm sugar, chopped
- 8 tbsp. thick tamarind water
- 6 tbsp. fish sauce

How to make it!

Heat the oil in a wok and deep-fry one by one the shallots, garlic, dried shrimp, chillies and galangal. Drain on a paper towel. Blend them all in a food processor. Add the shrimp paste, blend. Moisten with some oil used for deep-frying, up to 16 tablespoons, to smooth the progress of the blending. Bring this mixture to the boil in a pan. Season this with palm sugar, tamarind water and fish sauce. Simmer and stir regularly until it has a quite thick consistency, like jam. It should taste sweet, sour and salty. Adjust the seasoning if necessary.

On the road

Traveling by train is, next to flying, probably the safest and the most relaxed way to cover large distances in Thailand. Just north of Chinatown is the beautifully Thai Art Deco building of Bangkok's central train station. The old Hualamphong train station is in sheer contrast with the recently constructed and spotlessly clean underground that connects the train station with the city centres of Bangkok.

Contrast is a key word in Bangkok, it conveys its craziness and magic. You can have an exquisite 4000 Baht meal at a fine dining table on the 64th floor of a skyscraper (The Dome) and have an equally delicious 20 Baht dish on a plastic chair in a congested smoke-choked alley a few hours later.

I have always found airports and railway stations magical places. Places filled with the energy of change. Watching people on the move to a new part of their life or on their way back to what was before. In the departure hall of Hualamphong I stock up on a pile of deep-fried bananas ('kluay thod') for the train ride up north.

Another great thing about the departure hall of Hualamphong is that you can have a traditional massage on the mezzanine floor. Amazing Thailand!

There's a daily market (H) - except on Mondays, when they clean the pavement - a little north of Khao San Road, on Thanon Chakhraphong near the shopping mall. People that work in the area go there for a take-away lunch or dinner.

Every time I'm in Bangkok with visitors, I include a street food tour in that area. Here you get a good picture of what street food is all about. On a 100 meter stretch there are an estimated 100 different take-away dishes. I encourage my fellow travellers to try fishcakes ('thod man pla'), grilled fermented sausages ('sai krok'), grilled banana's ('kluay ping') and grilled sticky rice in banana leaf ('khao niaw ping').

Nobody in all the groups that I have guided around the street food stalls of Bangkok has ever fallen ill. The food hawker takes pride in the quality of his dishes. He goes daily to the food market to buy the day's ingredients. Usually, he finishes work when everything is sold out.

Area

BANGLAMPOO FOOD MARKET
136-40, Thanon Chakhraphong
Daily, closed on Sundays

This is a very cheap and filling snack. You receive it in a small plastic bag with a bamboo stick. Indicate if you want some dressing poured over it.

ทอดมันปลา

Fishcakes

thod man pla

You will see a lot of food vendors deep-frying these little delicacies. It's amazing to see them puff up. Eat them while they are still hot, they toughen as they cool.

Ingredients

- 300 g white fish fillets, chopped finely
- 4 tbsp. red curry paste
- 3 tbsp. fish sauce
- 1 egg, lightly beaten
- 1 tbsp. palm sugar or granulated sugar
- 5 kaffir lime leaves, deveined and shredded
- 2 tbsp. finely cut snake beans or green beans
- oil for deep-frying

How to make it!

Put all ingredients into a mixing bowl. Mix thoroughly (either use your hands, a pestle and mortar or a food processor) until you get a smooth paste. Take a large bowl, and throw the paste a few times back in the bowl. Continue until the mixture is firm. Doing this make the fishcakes not puff up when deep-fried. Divide in small portions and make small discs. Deep-fry until golden, drain and serve immediately with the cucumber relish.

Thai language is spiced up with hundreds of proverbs regarding food, more evidence of their passion and commitment to food. 'Nuad' is the Thai word for massage. That's exactly what they call the throwing of the fishcake to make it more firmly. Massaging fish cake!

อาจาด

Cucumber relish

naam jim taeng-gwa

Ingredients

- 4 tbsp. water
- 3 tbsp. sugar
- 3 tbsp. vinegar
- 1 pinch of salt
- ½ tsp. chilli powder or 1 large red chilli, julienned
- 4 tbsp. cucumber, julienned
- 2 tbsp. shallot, sliced
- 1 tbsp. coriander leaves, chopped

How to make it!

Bring water with sugar, vinegar and salt to the boil. Turn off the heat when sugar has dissolved. Cool. Add chilli, cucumber and shallot. Finish with coriander leaves.

This is a refreshing accompaniment; it works especially well with fish cakes. You can also add julienned ginger or coarsely chopped roasted peanuts if you want.

กล้วยทอด

Deep-fried banana

kluay thod

This filling snack is sold at virtually every train- and bus station. A lot of times, deep-fried pumpkin is on offer too.

Ingredients

- 6 small sweet bananas
- 200 g rice flour
- 200 g flour
- 1 tsp. baking soda
- 200 ml water
- 100 ml coconut milk
- ½ tsp. salt
- 50 g sesame seeds
- 3 tbsp. sugar
- 50 g coconut pulp
- oil for deep-frying

How to make it!

Peel the bananas and cut lengthwise in 4. Mix flour with the other ingredients. Dip the bananas into batter and deep-fry until golden.

ไส้กรอก
Grilled (fermented) sausages
sai krok

Ingredients
- 500 g minced pork
- 100 g sticky rice (optional)
- 5 coriander roots, chopped
- 6 garlic cloves, chopped
- 1 tbsp. salt
- 1 tbsp. fish sauce
- 1 tbsp. sugar
- sausage casing
- young ginger, diced / chilli, sliced in rings / roasted peanuts / iceberg lettuce

How to make it!
Steam the sticky rice for 20 minutes until cooked. Leave to cool.
Pound the coriander root, garlic and salt in a mortar into a smooth paste.
Add sticky rice and pork and season with fish sauce and sugar. Fill the casing with this mixture, make about 7 cm long sausages, and make a knot to finish each sausage.
Grill over charcoal for about 7 minutes until cooked, turning regularly.
Cut in pieces and eat together with some diced ginger, a (small) piece of chilli, some peanuts and some iceberg lettuce.

It's sometimes available in a fermented version. After preparations, they leave the sausages for a few days. Most foreigners are not used to this somewhat sour taste. In Thailand they use a grill shaped like the roof of a house (like a pyramid), so the fat can drip down.

Nowadays banana leaves are not so popular to wrap up food. This is one of the few dishes where it has not lost its packaging function. Maybe it's because of the delicious flavour of the banana leaf induced by grilling. Used often as a bite to go, carried as a type of lunch snack.

ข้าวเหนียวปิ้ง

Grilled sticky rice in banana leaf

khao niaw ping

Ingredients

- 1 large banana leaf
- 200 g sticky rice, soaked in cold water overnight or at least 3 hours in warm water
- wooden or bamboo skewers, soaked in water for at least 30 minutes

How to make it!

Hold the banana leaf over an open flame. This makes it supple and gives the leaf a beautiful dark green colour. Alternatively, the banana leaf can be blanched briefly in order to get the same result. Cut the leaf into rectangles (10 cm x 5 cm). Put 2 rectangles in a T-shape, top piece underneath. Steam the sticky rice for about 15 minutes until cooked. Leave to cool. Divide in small portions. Place a portion on the top piece of banana leaf. Fold in the edges and roll tightly. Secure with a skewer. Grill over charcoal for 6 minutes, turning regularly.

Fillings can be banana, taro, mung beans, black beans or shredded coconut. If you don't like surprises, point and ask for it 'sai arai khrap/ka', literally 'with what'.

กล้วยปิ้ง

Grilled banana

kluay ping

Be careful if you ask for grilled banana in Thai!
Wrong tone and you order a grilled penis.

Ingredients

- small banana
- sugar syrup

How to make it!

Grill the banana over charcoal for about 10 minutes.
Brush with sugar syrup and grill a bit longer.

Two kinds of banana are used: the sweet small banana ('kluay nam wa') is grilled unpeeled. The somewhat sour and bitter banana ('kluay huk muk') is grilled peeled. Both kinds are often sold by the same hawker. Sold also by the same hawker are grilled eggs, served with soy sauce ('kai ping'), steamed peanuts and steamed corn cobs.

Look out for this type of food vendor, a lot of times using a 'haph'. This way, the hawker sells his stuff and just walks away to the next customer.

Usually grilled yams or sweet potatoes will also be sold by the same food hawker. If you want to make it yourself, yams need at least 20 minutes on the grill.

One-dish-wonders

When Thai people travel they make sure that there is plenty of food at hand. Transport hubs are almost like food fairs in Thailand. Somehow I always seem to find a place that sells stewed pork on rice ('khao kha moo') in these areas, although you can find it at numerous food markets. The fragrance of the cinnamon, cloves and star anise is so typical for this preparation that you can smell the dish from afar. This is not an obvious dish to sample as it doesn't look that appealing. The taste on the other hand is something I long for when I'm at home in Belgium.

Another place for some of the finest traditional Thai food is 'Krua Aroi Aroi' (14). 'Krua' is the Thai word for 'kitchen' and 'aroi' means 'delicious'. By repeating a word twice in Thai you stress its meaning.

I remember one time cycling from the Thewet area up north to this place. It's just across from one of the most spectacular Hindu temples in Thailand (Sri Mariamman or Wat Khaek).

OK, it's madness to cycle in Bangkok but for good food I'll go a long way. On my first visit, I had a northern dish of chicken in curry broth and deep-fried noodles ('kao soi gai'). The Indian influence is notable in this dish. Its origin is related to Muslim traders who were passing through northern Thailand on their way to China.

When I biked back to my guesthouse, my face sweaty and blackened from exhaust fumes, I was grateful to have survived and swore not to tell my mom I was cycling in Bangkok. On a second visit I was smart enough to grab an air-conditioned taxi, infused with the smells of jasmine flower. The woman at 'Krua Aroi Aroi' recognised me immediately and helped me through their menu. She encouraged me to try the 'khanom jeen', a traditional dish that comes in many varieties.

14

Address

KRUA AROI AROI
Thanon Pan, off Silom Road,
just across the Indian Temple, Wat Khaek
Open: 10:00 – 18:00, daily

ข้าวซอยไก่

Chiang Mai Chicken

kao soi gai

This is a wonderful complete dish, in which the deep-fried noodles form an exceptional contrast with the smooth texture of the soup.

Ingredients

- 2 chicken legs
- 4 tbsp. coconut cream
- 1 tbsp. palm sugar
- 2 tbsp. light soy sauce
- 1 tsp. dark soy sauce
- 500 ml chicken stock
- 1 handful of fresh egg noodles
- a few deep-fried egg noodles
- 2 spring onion, chopped
- 1 handful of chopped coriander leaves

(Paste)

- 3 big, red, dried chillies, deseeded, soaked in water for 10 minutes, drained, chopped
- 2 red shallots, chopped
- 1 tsp. coriander seed, roasted
- 2 garlic cloves, chopped
- 2 cm turmeric, chopped
- 2 cm ginger, chopped
- 3 coriander roots, scraped and chopped
- 1 pinch of salt

(To serve with)

- pickled vegetables
- 1 shallot, sliced finely
- 1 lime, cut in wedges

How to make it!

Pound the paste ingredients together, using a pestle and mortar, until smooth. Simmer the coconut cream in a pan until the oil starts to separate. Turn down the heat and add the paste. Fry the paste in the oil for 5 minutes. Add the chicken and simmer. Season with palm sugar, light and dark soy sauce. Moisten with stock and simmer for about 20 minutes, the chicken should be cooked.

Blanch the egg noodles, put into a bowl, top with the chicken and pour over the soup. Top it with deep-fried egg noodles and garnish with spring onion and coriander. Serve with pickled vegetables, slices of shallot and wedges of lime.

You can find variations on this dish (for instance with beef) but never with pork since originally it's a Muslim dish.

There are a lot of secret recipes for this dish. Every food vendor has improved his or her recipe to perfection, often over generations. A small serving of raw garlic cloves and small chilli peppers comes with every portion. Just take a bit of both on your spoon, together with the food. This will help to break down the fat.

ข้าวขาหมู

Stewed pork on rice

khao kha moo

We know, it looks rather appalling at first but do try it. The meat is utterly succulent and the five-spice powder gives it an astonishing aroma.

Ingredients

- 2 tsp. black peppercorns
- 1 tsp. salt
- 6 garlic cloves, chopped
- 4 coriander roots, scraped and chopped
- 2 tbsp. vegetable oil
- 4 tbsp. palm sugar
- 1 tbsp. water
- 1 kg pork leg, shaved and cleaned
- enough water to cover
- 1 tsp. dark soy sauce
- 4 tbsp. soy sauce
- 1 nutmeg
- 3 cloves
- 3 star anise
- 4 cm cinnamon stick
- ½ tsp. five-spices-powder
- 4 eggs, hardboiled, peeled

(Sauce)

- 2 medium chillies
- 1 coriander root, scraped and chopped very finely
- 2 garlic cloves, chopped finely
- ½ tsp. salt
- 2 tbsp. vinegar

(To serve with)

- steamed or stir-fried greens (e.g. Chinese broccoli, spinach, pak choi)
- cooked rice

How to make it!

Pound the peppercorns with salt in a mortar, until the peppercorns are completely pulverised. Add coriander root and garlic whilst pounding. The result should be a smooth, fragrant paste. In a large pan, heat the oil on a medium heat. Fry the paste until all the smells are distinguishable. Add the palm sugar and lower the heat. The sugar has to melt, not burn. Stir, add 1 tbsp. of water and keep stirring. Prick a few times with a fork in the pork leg and add it too, make sure the leg is completely covered with the sauce. >>

Stewed pork on rice

Thai people are fond of the fat. Often they even consider it the better piece and if they want to please you, they make sure you get a fair portion of it. If you don't share this liking, say 'kho mai sai man kalkrap.' I don't want the fat, please.

>> If the pan is not big enough, transfer everything to a large pot, add water so that everything is covered. Turn the heat to medium. Add the soy sauces, nutmeg, cloves, star anise, cinnamon, five-spices-powder and eggs. Cover with a lid and bring to the boil. When boiling, remove the lid and spoon off the foam. Keep simmering on a low heat for 2-3 hours until the meat is tender. Turn regularly.

In the meantime, pound the chillies, coriander root, garlic and salt in a mortar. Stir in the vinegar and set aside. Cut the pork in bite-sized strips and serve on top of rice. Quarter the eggs and put some of them next to it. Serve with the greens and a small bowl of sauce.

ขนมจีนน้ำพริก

Thin rice noodles with spicy shrimp and coconut

khanom jeen nam phrik

Khanom jeen food vendors are increasingly hard to find since most preparations are very elaborate. They will have different sauces to choose from, so try a few and enjoy.

Ingredients

- 400 g khanom jeen noodles or very thin dried rice noodles, spaghetti-like
- 2 shallots, unpeeled
- 2 garlic cloves, unpeeled
- 1 knob galangal, unpeeled
- 1 coriander root, scraped and chopped
- 1 tsp. salt
- 1 can of coconut milk (400 ml)
- 4 tbsp. vegetable oil
- 2-3 tsp. chilli powder
- 200 ml water
- 250 g prawns, peeled and deveined
- 6 tbsp. unsalted roasted peanuts, chopped
- 6 tbsp. roasted coconut flakes
- 2 tbsp. mung beans, roasted and ground
- 4 tbsp. palm sugar
- 4 tbsp. fish sauce
- 3 tbsp. lime juice

(Accompaniments)

- soy bean sprouts
- hardboiled eggs
- ¼ small banana flower, cut into strips, soaked in water with some lime juice
- sliced green beans
- boiled cabbage
- tempura vegetables
- pickled vegetables
- fried garlic
- wedges of lime

How to make it!

Khanom jeen noodles are semi-fermented rice noodles, which can only be found in Thailand. Substitute with dried rice noodles, cook following the instructions on the package. Rinse with cold water, drain and set aside. >>

Thin rice noodles with spicy shrimp and coconut

>> Roast the shallots, garlic and galangal in a very hot oven, maximum degrees. Peel, chop finely and pound in a mortar with coriander root and salt until smooth. Set aside.
Do not shake the can, the top layer is coconut cream, the bottom layer is coconut milk. Spoon out the cream and set aside. Heat the oil in a wok over medium heat, stir in the reserved paste and fry until fragrant. This should take about 2 minutes. Add the coconut cream and keep stirring for about 4-5 minutes. You will see that the oil will start to separate. Add the chilli powder, little by little, adding more according to preferable spiciness. Keep stirring briefly until everything is mixed well, turn off the heat.

Pour the coconut milk into a pot and add water. Bring to the boil and poach the prawns until they change colour, about 2 minutes. Remove the prawns with a slotted spoon and grind roughly two-thirds of it in a food processor or pound coarsely in a mortar. Combine the ground and the whole and set aside.Add the chilli paste mixture to the coconut milk. Add the peanuts and about 4 tablespoons of the roasted coconut flakes. Mix in the mung beans, prawns, palm sugar and fish sauce. Turn off the heat and add the lime juice.

Taste, it should be sweet, sour, salty and spicy. Adjust if needed. Before serving, mix in the remaining roasted coconut flakes. Serve small coils of noodles at room temperature on a plate with accompaniments and sauce to your liking.

Literally translated 'khanom' means 'pastry'. This translation causes confusion with people unfamiliar with 'khanom jeen'. They expect a dessert or at least something sweet and they get a savoury noodle dish accompanied by many small dishes.
There are countless variations and recipes in the running. Some include fish balls, others pork, seafood or dried fish.

Khao San Road is a colourful and lively area where backpackers from around the globe gather to exchange information… and much more.

On my first visits to Bangkok, I stayed in and around this area a few times and I quickly discovered Roti Mataba (15) on Phra Sumen Road. This is a fine example of the Indian immigrant, getting famous for his food in Thailand. Just after World War II, he began selling his dishes at a food stall. Forty years later, he was able to open a small restaurant. Nowadays the place is always packed. If you fancy something different, try this place as they do good Muslim food. I used to order the roti with banana and condensed milk - take-away ('sai tung') – and eat it in the riverfront park across the street.

15

Address

ROTI MATABA
136, Phra Athit Road,
opposite Phra Sumen fort
Open: 07:00 – 22:00,
closed on Mondays

โรตี

Roti

roti

Ingredients

- 250 g all-purpose flour
- 1 pinch of salt
- 1 pinch of sugar
- 1 egg, lightly beaten
- 2 tbsp. water
- ghee for frying

How to make it!

Combine the flour, salt, sugar, egg and water. Knead the dough until firm. Divide into lime-sized balls as set aside to stand, covered with a damp cloth, for at least 30 minutes. Roll a dough ball flat, maximum 1 cm thick. Pick up disc, twist to make a rope, wrap into a spiral. Roll the spiral flat again into discs. Fry disc in the ghee over a low heat, about 4 minutes each side. Repeat with the other dough balls.

One of my recent discoveries, but a place that has been around a long time, is 'Thip Samai' (16). Years ago, when I tried to find it, some dodgy Thai person, whom I asked for directions, took me to his friend's restaurant for the 'real phat thai'. After being fooled, I gave up searching.

On a second attempt, I discovered out that it opens only at six o'clock in the evening, since I was standing in front thirty minutes before that, when they were cleaning tables. I waited and relaxed nearby on the temple grounds of the Golden Mount Temple. When I finally got in half an hour later the place was packed at once, people kept queuing outside next to the steaming red woks with fried noodles ('phat thai'). I sat alone at a table and ordered a 'phat thai' with green mango and crab. I looked around and I suddenly felt a little silly eating there all by myself. Thai food is something you eat with friends and I had the sudden sad feeling everybody else knew so too.

It opened in 1966 and they owe their success to the continuous care for only the best ingredients and the loyalty that they show to their customers. Mrs. Samai started originally in the Maha Chai district and later moved to Bangkok. Because of the rainy season the owner later opened up the restaurant in a house. It's probably the best known and cleanest 'phat thai' place in town. They charge thrice the price of a 'phat thai' down the road but it's worth it, every single Baht. The varieties include 'phat thai' wrapped in egg and 'phat thai' with green mango and crab. The dishes come with sliced banana flower, soybeans and fresh spring union. Spice it up with chilli flakes, fish sauce and grilled grounded peanuts.

When cooked on a hot plate, there's a fair chance that he or she will also sell mussel pancakes ('hoi thod') as mainly the same basic ingredients are used. Already more than seventy years in business and still going strong is 'Thip Vulcanic Fried Mussel & Oyster' (17).

16

Address

THIP SAMAI
313, Mahachai Road Samranrat, Pranakorn
Open: 18:00 – 24:00, daily
www.thipsamai.com

17

Address

THIP VOLCANIC FRIED MUSSEL & OYSTER
3, Charoen Krung Soi 50, near Robinson Bangrak
Open: 09:00 – 19:00, closed on Sundays

A lot of 'phat thai' vendors use a hot plate to make it on, since it's easier to handle and larger quantities can be made. For best results however, you have to use a wok.

'Phat thai became popular during the war in Vietnam, when a lot of American soldiers came to R&R in Thailand. That's why some food vendors started to add ketchup to it. Luckily that variation didn't last very long.

ผัดไทย

Stir-fried noodles with prawns

phat thai

In fact, this is derived from a Chinese dish but after a few Thai modifications (adding tamarind water for instance) this is regarded as a very Thai dish.

Ingredients

- 4 tbsp. fish sauce
- 2 tbsp. palm sugar
- 2 tbsp. white sugar
- 2 tbsp. tamarind water
- 250 g thin dried rice noodles, soaked for 1-2 hours in water
- 3 tbsp. vegetable oil
- 2 shallots, chopped finely
- 2 garlic cloves, chopped finely
- 3 tbsp. dried baby shrimps
- 1 egg, lightly beaten
- 4 tbsp. firm tofu, deep-fried and diced in small cubes
- 2 tbsp. pickled radish, chopped
- 1 tsp. chilli powder
- 1 small bunch of Chinese chives, chopped into 2 cm lengths
- 1 handful of soy bean sprouts

(Accompaniments)

- 1 handful of soy bean sprouts
- a few sprigs of Chinese chives, chopped in 5 cm length
- ¼ small banana flower, cut into strips, soaked in water with some lime juice
- 1 lime, cut in wedges
- 4 tbsp. roasted peanuts, ground roughly
- extra sugar
- extra chilli powder

How to make it!

Simmer the fish sauce, palm sugar, white sugar and tamarind water until sugar is dissolved. Set aside. Drain noodles. Heat the oil in a wok over a medium heat and gradually fry the shallots, garlic and dried shrimps. Add egg, turn heat on low and keep stirring. Add tofu and white radish, and then add the noodles. Turn up the heat and make sure that the noodles are evenly coated. Mix in the prepared sauce and the chilli powder whilst stirring. Add the Chinese chives and the bean sprouts. Put on a plate and serve with accompaniments.

หอยทอด

Mussel pancake

hoi thod

Try this after a night of drinking to alleviate your hangover the day after.

Ingredients

- 500 g mussels, scrubbed and shelled
- 2 tbsp. vegetable oil
- 1 egg, lightly beaten
- 1 handful of soy bean sprouts
- 1 spring onion, chopped
- 1 tbsp. light soy sauce
- 1 tbsp. fish sauce
- 1 tsp. sugar
- 1 handful of coriander leaves
- 1 pinch of white pepper

(Batter)

- 3 tbsp. rice flour
- 3 tbsp. flour
- 1 pinch of salt
- 1 egg
- 200 ml water

How to make it!

First make the batter by thoroughly mixing all the ingredients. Add the mussels and set aside. Heat a plate or a wide flat pan with oil and ladle in the batter to make a pancake. When the pancake begins to look crusty around the outside, flip it to cook the other side.

Break up the pancake and fry the egg in between. Add soy bean sprouts and spring onion and stir well. Add soy sauce, fish sauce and sugar to season and garnish with the coriander leaves and pepper.

Serve with sweet chilli sauce.

Perfect for a picnic

The Thais must be the world's most picnic-loving people. Every occasion is a reason to bring out the mats to relax and eat. That's what Thai people like to do most, come together, have fun ('sanuk'), talk, drink and eat. You have got to hand it to them; they have a joie de vivre, a zest for living.

On this lazy day I'm meeting my friend in the Chatuchak Park. Before heading down there, I make a stop at the 'Or-Tor-Kor' (I) food market just across. This market is a chef's paradise, high quality products from all over Thailand, all stacked under one roof. Hi-so (high society) ladies and their housemaids come here to shop for the best ingredients. I still have half an hour to kill and I'm feeling slightly hungry.

Before I take a walk through the wet market, I have some grilled sausages ('sai oea') at the food court at the back of the market. It's wise to eat before you go shopping at a food market or you end up with half the market in your fridge. After finishing this savoury snack, I take a stroll through the market and buy some 'miang kam', a perfect snack for a picnic in the park. This market is truly awesome.

I

Area

OR-TOR-KOR FOOD MARKET
Thanon Kamphaengphet
Open: daily from 06:00 till 18:00

Everything is so hard to resist at this market. At the ready-made food section, I can't stop myself buying some more for our little food party in the park. For a brief moment, I hesitate between the grilled fish in salt crust ('pla pao') and the deep-fried snapper ('pla thod'). But as I know my friend is keener on sweet things, I buy the deep-fried fish with sweet sauce.

ปลาเผา

Grilled fish in salt

pla pao

Amazingly simple, less is more.

Ingredients

- 1 sea bass
- 4 stalks of lemongrass
- 250 g coarse sea salt

How to make it!

First clean the fish (scaled, eviscerated and washed), pat dry. Cut of the hard bottom end of the lemongrass, bruise with a knife to release all the flavour.

Stick the stalks of lemongrass through the fish via its mouth, this makes a kind of herbal skewer. Cover both sides with salt. Grill over charcoal for about 15 to 20 minutes, turning regularly until cooked.

The lime-chilli-dressing ('naam jim thaleh') goes well with this. Lemongrass is a superb stuffing for fish, it adds a distinctive freshness.

Since this is a northern dish, it is usually served with sticky rice. In the north of Thailand, red curry paste is often added to the sausage mixture for extra flavour and spiciness.

ไส้อั่ว

Grilled sausages from the north of Thailand

sai oea

Most foreigners prefer these sausages over 'sai krok'. The taste of the lemongrass, galangal and kaffir lime leave is divine.

Ingredients

- 500 g minced pork
- 5 coriander roots, chopped
- 6 garlic cloves, chopped
- 1 tbsp. salt
- 1 tsp. ground black pepper
- 1 tbsp. lemongrass, chopped
- 2 tsp. galangal, chopped
- 1 shallot, chopped
- 1 tsp. shrimp paste
- 2 medium chillies, chopped
- 3 kaffir lime leaves, chopped very finely - sausage casing

How to make it!

Combine all the ingredients. Put the mixture in the casing making small sausages and make a knot to finish each sausage. Grill over charcoal about 7 minutes, turning regularly.

ปลาทอด

Deep-fried fish

pla thod

Ingredients

- 1 small sea bass, sea bream
- 1-2 tbsp. fish sauce or light soy sauce
- 1 pinch of salt
- 1 pinch of sugar
- 1 large pinch of white pepper
- oil for deep-frying

How to make it!

Clean the fish (scaled, eviscerated and washed), pat dry with paper towel. Make diagonal cuts into the bass, both sides. Marinate the fish overnight in fish sauce or soy sauce, salt, sugar and pepper. Remove and leave to dry for at least an hour. Deep-fry until crispy. Drain and leave to stand several minutes before serving.

If you don't have time to marinate the fish, go for the quick version: marinate the fish in fish sauce or soy sauce for about 10 minutes. Drain and deep-fry until crispy. This is a basic recipe for deep-fried fish; you can serve it with a dip or with garlic and pepper, sweet chilli sauce, etc.

You can find this snack pre-packed on the streets of Bangkok, usually all ingredients packed separately in small plastic bags. Variations can be made. Add pomelo, fresh oysters or mussels to the array of filling ingredients.

เมี่ยงคำ

Leaf-wrapped bits

miang kum

Miang kam is a prime example of Thai cuisine, a perfect balance of different flavours all combined in one.

Ingredients

- 16 betel leaves ('bai champluu') or young spinach leaves
- 1 tbsp. diced lime
- 2 tbsp. grated coconut, roasted
- 2 tbsp. roasted peanuts
- 1 tbsp. diced young ginger
- 2 tbsp. dried baby shrimps, roasted
- 2 tbsp. diced shallots
- 1-3 small chillis, finely sliced in rings

(Paste)

- 4 slices galangal, roasted
- 1 large pinch of salt
- 2 small chillies
- ½ tsp. shrimp paste, roasted
- 1 tbsp. dried baby shrimp, ground
- 3 tbsp. grated coconut, roasted
- 1 tbsp. peanuts, roasted and ground

(Sauce)

- 5 tbsp. palm sugar
- 75 ml water
- 4 tbsp. fish sauce
- 3 tbsp. tamarind water

How to make it!

For the paste, pound the ingredients together in a mortar, adding them one by one, until smooth. For the sauce, heat the sugar with water. When the sugar is dissolved, let simmer for several minutes until it thickens. Add fish sauce, then stir in the paste and continue to simmer for a few minutes. You should be able to smell the galangal. Add the tamarind water and put on a low heat. Keep simmering for a few more minutes. Remove from the heat. Leave to cool.

How to serve it!

Put the leaves in the middle of a plate and present little piles of the lime, coconut, peanuts, ginger, shrimp, shallot and chilli around them. Every guest can take a leaf, fold it like a small envelop, fill it with the ingredients according to personal taste, top it with some sauce, close it and eat it in one go. It's important that you don't bite it in two but put it as one piece in your mouth. This is to insure that you have all the taste layers together.

Late night

When I get back to the Thewet area at night my friends still hang out on the streets playing guitar, chatting and drinking. It's hard to pass them without stopping for a nightcap.

I see Ash, who has been a great source of information and a partner in discussing Asian politics over the past few years. Neil is around as well, a former teacher in England who's working on a novel. 'Did anyone see Indian Steve?' someone asks.

Apparently, he's gone back to India, according to Pui. Thewet is the centre of the world!

As we are getting drunk on Beer Chang, I promise myself that this beer is going to be the last one. The dried squid seller passes by on his bicycle. 'Pla muek ping' sellers are always on the move, on bicycles or on boats but never fixed to one location. These days dried squid sellers are becoming a rarity. I pick out a few dried squid from his rack that is attached to his bicycle; he flattens them through a hand cracked press and grills them for a few minutes over a charcoal fire. It is perfect drinking food as the salt mixes well with beer. Chips avant-la-lettre!

Tel. (02)2808858-8

ปลาหมึกย่าง

Grilled dried squid

pla muek yang

Listen for that unique tune and if you are lucky to spot one, order a portion, and enjoy it while you still can.

Ingredients

- 1 fresh middle-sized squid, cleaned
- 250 g salt

How to make it!

Rub in the squid vigorously with the salt and leave to dry in the sun or at least 2 hours in an oven (100°C).
Flatten the squid in a press. Alternatively you can use a pasta machine.
Grill the squid over charcoal, about 3 minutes each side.

Once ordered, you get your serving in a piece of newspaper, folded into a bag, together with a sweet chilli dip and/or a sweet dip with peanuts. The sweetness balances the saltiness extraordinarily well.

The night has ended at the market, playing snooker at a pool table in the middle of the market. Luckily I went to bed when others went to buy flowers at the Pak Khlong Talaad flower market at five o'clock in the morning.

The hangover is probably the same. I need food. Just when I'm walking out of the guesthouse at noon a mobile cart passes by and a new day begins.

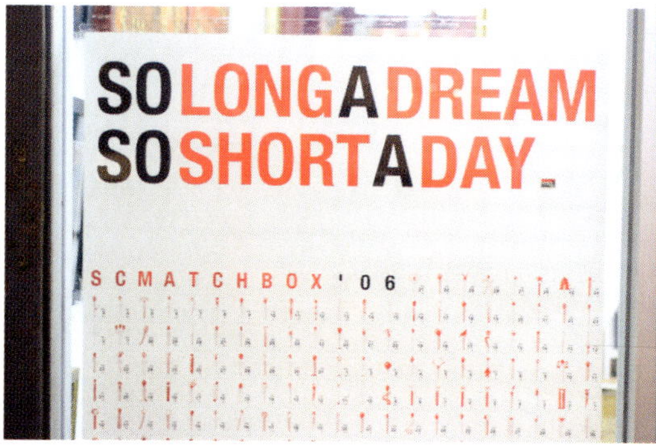

Addresses

RESTAURANTS

1 **Rice soup ('Joak') food stall**
Address: corner of Soi Rambutri and Tanao Road in front of '7-Eleven'
Open: 18:00 – 23:00, daily

2 **Namtok Sida**
Address: Wang Lang market (go left along Wang Lang,
turn right in Trok Wang Lang, next to a shop called Wienna)
Open: 09:00 – 18:00, closed on Sundays

3 **Khao Tom Polo**
Address: Corner of Wireless Road and Soi Sanam Khli (Soi Polo) 137/14,
near Lumphini police station
Open: 18:00 – 22:00, closed on Sundays

4 **Raat Na Yod Pak**
Address: Tanao Road, on right side between Thanon Phreang Sanphasat
and Thanon Phreang Nara
Open: 09:00 – 21:00, daily

5 **Gai Yang Boran**
Address: 474-476, Tanao Road
Open: 09:00 – 20:00, daily

6 **Chote Chitr**
Address: 146, Prang Pu Thorn, off Tanao Road
Open: 11:00 – 23:00, closed on Sundays

7 **Kao Niaw Kor Panich**
Address: 431-433, Tanao Road
Open: 6:30 –19:30, June through December: closed on Sundays

8 **Mon Nom Sod 1**
Address: 160/2-3, Dinso Road
Open: 14:00 – 24:00, daily

9 **Khanom Buang**
Address: 100-102, Phra Sumen Road, on your right side, coming from the fort,
halfway between Phra Athit Road and Samsen Road
Open: 09:00 – 18:00, closed on Sundays

10 **Khanom Buang Phraeng Nara**
Address: Tanao Road, on your right side, walking down from Ratchadamnoen Avenue
Open: 10:00 – 18:00, closed on Sundays

11 **Gai ton Pratunam**
Address: 30, Petchaburi Road Soi, opposite Pratunam Plaza, Pratunam
Open: 18:00 – 2:00, daily

12 **Pet Tun Jao**
Address: 945, Soi Wanit 2, near the Harbour Department building
Open: 10:30 – 17:00, closed on Sundays

13 **T & K Seafood**
Address: 49-51, Phadung Dao Road (Soi Texas), corner of Yawalat Road and Soi Texas
Open: 16:30 – 24:00, daily

14 **Krua Aroi Aroi**
Address: Thanon Pan, off Silom Road, just across the Indian Temple, Wat Khaek
Open: 10:00 – 18:00, daily

15 **Roti Mataba**
Address: 136, Phra Athit Road, opposite Phra Sumen fort
Open: 07:00 – 22:00, closed on Mondays

16 **Thip Samai**
Address: 313, Mahachai Road, Samranrat, Pranakorn
Open: 18:00 – 24:00, daily
www.thipsamai.com

17 **Thip Volcanic Fried Mussel & Oyster**
Address: 3, Charoen Krung Soi 50, near Robinson Bangrak
Open: 09:00 – 19:00, closed on Sundays

MARKETS AND FOODRELATED AREA'S

A **Thewet area and Thewet food market**, great for breakfast and lunch on weekdays and for the lively and authentic food market early in the morning along the canal and Samsen Road
Address: Sri Ayudhaya Road, Soi 12
Chao Phraya Express boat pier: Tha Thewez

B **Pak Khlong Talaat, wholesale vegetable market and flower market**, at its best early morning from 04:00 – 10:00, great for Thai donuts ('pah tong koh'), soy milk and coffee.
Address: Maharat Road near Memorial Bridge
Chao Phraya Express boat pier: Tha Rachani

C **Wang Lang market,** with second hand and new clothes and lots of food on offer, starts at 10:00 till 18:00, take-away food such as steamed fishcakes ('ha mok') and deep-fried spring rolls ('pah piah tod').
Address: next to Siriraj Hospital
Chao Phraya Express boat pier: Tha Wang Lang

D **Amulet market**, great for authentic amulets and lunch at riverfront restaurant, try the well-known dish ('yam pla duk foo'), look for the sponge-like deep-fried fish in glass showcases, starts at 10:00 till 17:00.
Address: Maharat Road and Pra Chan Road
Chao Phraya Express boat pier: Tha Pra Chan

E **Soachingcha**, famous area for street food on weekdays, look for thick noodles in gravy ('raat na') in a place called 'Raat Na Yod Pak' and for grilled chicken ('gai yang') in 'Gai Yang Boran'.
Address: along Tanao Road and Dinso Road

F **Old Siam Plaza**, ground floor of one of the first shopping malls in Bangkok, legendary sweets and desserts, great place to watch people making golden threads ('foi tong'), open from 09:00 – 21:00
Address: Burapha Road, Phranakorn, near Little India

G **Chinatown**, superb street food in the evening, starts around 18:00 till midnight
Address: Yawalat Road and side roads.

H **Banglampoo food market**, every day – except Sundays and sometimes Mondays, there's a food market along Thanon Chakhraphong Road, just north of Khao San Road with a wide variety of snacks available; look out for the renowned curry paste shop Nittaya
Address: 136-40, Thanon Chakhraphong

I **Or-Tor-Kor food market**, just behind the famous Chatuchak market (JJ market), top quality ingredients, a must see for every chef, dining area in the back, open daily from 06:00 till 18:00
Address: Thanon Kamphaengphet

Language

Thai is a tonal language and thus extremely difficult to learn. Five different tones are used: low (à), middle, high (á), falling (â) and rising (ã). The meaning of a single syllable can be altered in five different ways. Here is an example with four tones and one syllable: 'mái mài mâi mãi', means 'new word burns, doesn't it'.

In our experience, the right word in the wrong tone is not understood or 'automatically corrected' by Thai people. This can lead to hilarious or frustrating experiences, depending on your attitude. Be patient, remember that you are the tourist, you are visiting them. Sometimes a lot of gesticulation can also be a way of communicating.

However, if you do make an effort, you will notice that a few words of Thai vocabulary will make a difference! In the cities English is widely spoken, but if you really want to discover hidden gems, try to master some Thai. You will be rewarded with excellent treats!

Important: if you're a man, you should end your sentence with 'khráp'. Woman use 'khâ'. There is not a literal translation but these syllables expresses politeness.

English	Phonetic Thai	Thai
Hello	Sawàt dee	สวัสดี
How are you	Sàbai dee mãi	สบายดีไหม
I'm fine	Sàbai dee	สบายดี
Thank you	Khòp khun	ขอบคุณ
Good luck/cheers	Chôk dee	โชคดี
No problem/it's ok/ never mind	Mâi pen rai	ไม่เป็นไร
I understand	Khâo jai	เข้าใจ
I don't understand	Mâi khâo jai	ไม่เข้าใจ
This, here	Têe nêe	ที่นี่
There	Têe nân	ที่นั่น
Over there	Têe nôhn	ที่โน่น
What	Àrai	อะไร
How much is...?	Tâo rài	เท่าไหร่
Do you have...?	Mii ... mãi	มี... ไหม
Can I...?	Dâai ... mãi	ได้... ไหม
I would like to...	Yàak jà ...	อยากจะ...
I like...	Cháwp ...	ชอบ...
To eat	Kin khâo	กินข้าว
Good	Dee	ดี
Bad	Mâi dee	ไม่ดี
Delicious	Àroî	อร่อย
Difficult	Yâak	ยาก
Easy	Mâi yâak	ไม่ยาก
Spicy	Pèt	เผ็ด

Index

B

C

M

N

P

R

S

V

W

colophon

Bangkok Street Food
Copyright © 2009 Lannoo Publishers, Belgium

Published in Asia in 2011 by
Page One Publishing Pte Ltd
20 Kaki Bukit View
Kaki Bukit Techpark II
Singapore 415956
Tel: [65] 6742-2088
Fax: [65] 6744-2088
enquiries@pageonegroup.com
www.pageonegroup.com

First published 2009 by Lannoo Publishers, Belgium

Text: copyright © 2009 Tom Vandenberghe & Eva Verplaetse, www.eetavontuur.be
Images: copyright © 2009 Luk Thys, www.foodphoto.be
Food styling: Els Goethals, www.elzasfood.be
Design & Lay-out: copyright © 2009 Quatre Mains, www.quatremains.be

ISBN: 978-981-275-261-1

All rights reserved. No part of this publication may be reproduced, stored in any retrieval system or transmitted, in any form or by any means, electronic, mechanical, photocopying, recording or otherwise, without prior permission in writing from the publisher. For information, contact Page One Publishing Pte Ltd.

Printed in Slovenia